William Henry Howell

Dissection of the Dog

As a Basis for the Study of Physiology

William Henry Howell

Dissection of the Dog
As a Basis for the Study of Physiology

ISBN/EAN: 9783337253608

Printed in Europe, USA, Canada, Australia, Japan

Cover: Foto ©Thomas Meinert / pixelio.de

More available books at **www.hansebooks.com**

AS A BASIS FOR THE STUDY OF PHYSIOLOGY

BY

W. H. HOWELL, A.B., PH.D.

LECTURER IN PHYSIOLOGY AND HISTOLOGY IN THE UNIVERSITY OF MICHIGAN, FORMERLY
ASSOCIATE IN BIOLOGY, JOHNS HOPKINS UNIVERSITY

NEW YORK

HENRY HOLT AND COMPANY

1889

TABLE OF CONTENTS.

INTRODUCTION.

PREFACE.

It is admitted beyond all question that even an elementary study of human physiology ought to be preceded by a more or less thorough dissection of some mammal. This little book, prepared originally for the author's own class, is intended to give this necessary anatomical basis to those who have not the opportunity of dissecting the human body. With this purpose in view, attention has been directed to those organs which are the chief objects of physiological study, rather than to those which have mainly an anatomical interest. One chapter has been inserted treating of the anatomy of the muscles of the shoulder and arm, but the author does not think it advisable to require this of a class unless there is abundance of time at the teacher's disposal. The anatomy of these muscles is of no particular importance in general physiology, and even from the standpoint of comparative anatomy it has but little value owing to the incomplete knowledge possessed with regard to muscle homologies among the mammalia. With reference to the muscles of the abdomen and the thorax the case is very different: these muscles play an important part in the performance of the respiratory movements, and their position and relations ought to be known by the student. Descriptions of these muscles, therefore, have been inserted in connection with the chapters on the abdominal and thoracic viscera.

The dog has been selected in preference to the rabbit or the cat, the other animals usually employed for such purposes, for several reasons. In most respects its anatomy corresponds very closely to that of man ; the size of the blood-vessels and other organs is relatively large, and this is especially true of the thoracic viscera and the neck region, which can be dissected with more success by the beginner upon the dog than upon the rabbit or the cat; if small dogs are selected, they will be found to be of a convenient size for general laboratory use ; finally, most of the usual physiological experiments and demonstrations are made upon the dog, and a knowledge of its anatomy will therefore prove particularly valuable to those who intend to make a special study of physiology.

The directions for dissection have been divided into seven chapters, with the idea that a fresh dog would be used for each chapter with the exception of those upon the muscles of the shoulder and arm, the brain, and the eye, requiring therefore four dogs for the entire work, though a smaller number may be made to answer. To obtain the most satisfactory results, however, one must be careful not to attempt to dissect too much upon a single animal. When the student is at work upon the blood-vessels he should not be required to dissect at the same time the peripheral nervous system. A much better knowledge of the circulatory organs, especially of their relations to each other, will be obtained if they are dissected as a whole. After learning the anatomy of the blood-vessels the nerves can be dissected with greater success, and their relations to the arteries and veins determined more easily.

The same remarks apply of course to other groups of organs. Each chapter, therefore, with the exceptions named, has been arranged so as to include a number of regions or sets of organs which can be conveniently dissected upon one animal. If there is not sufficient time for a class to do the whole chapter, there is no obstacle in the way to prevent the teacher from selecting the most important parts and omitting the others.

In the use of terms denoting directions and relations it has been thought best to employ the usual nomenclature rather than to adopt the more recent and more exact designations proposed by various authors. These latter are not as yet current in general anatomical literature or standard anatomies; indeed it remains to be seen which of those proposed will prove "the fittest." It did not seem wise, then, to burden the beginner with a discussion as to the use of terms, when in the great majority of cases the terms in ordinary use are sufficiently definite. The terms of direction made use of are: anterior, meaning toward the head; posterior, toward the tail; dorsal and ventral, with the usual significance; and right and left, inner and outer, with reference to the mid-line of the body.

In the directions for dissecting and in the descriptive part of the text an effort has been made to avoid unnecessary minuteness in the instructions. To a person altogether ignorant of the methods of dissecting a written description cannot fully supply the place of an instructor; it is necessary and indeed better for him to learn some things from experience. To students with some little experience in the art of dissection, or working under the guidance of an instructor, it is a hindrance rather than an advantage to attempt to describe just the direction and extent of each cut, the way in which the instruments should be held, etc., or to point out all the numerous possible mistakes which may be made. It is better to leave something to the intelligence and discretion of the teacher or the pupil, if the dissecting is to prove a healthy discipline.

It is but proper to say that the general idea of the arrangement of the directions for dissection was taken from the very excellent book on "Practical Zoology" by Marshall and Hurst.

I take pleasure also in expressing my thanks to my friend Mr. T. D. Coleman, Assistant in Physiology in this laboratory, for his kindness in helping me in the dissections and in the preparation of the diagrams.

W. H. Howell.

Johns Hopkins University,
Baltimore, Md.

INTRODUCTION.

THE following brief description of methods and instruments may contain some useful practical hints for those whose experience in such matters is limited.

Method of Killing and Preparing the Dog.—The quickest and most merciful method of killing the dog is to chloroform him. For this purpose it is only necessary to have a tight box or metal can with a well-fitting cover. In the bottom of this box place a sponge saturated with chloroform, put in the dog and close the lid. After a short time the animal becomes quiet, but it should not be removed from the box until all respiratory movements have ceased. For convenience in dissecting the dog should then be tied down upon some form of dog-holder. Perhaps the simplest and most economical form, one which can be readily made and answers every purpose, is shown in I, Fig. 1. It consists of a board about 30 inches long and 12 inches wide, supported upon two blocks, and having at one end a piece of bent iron rod which can be fastened into the mouth, and serves to hold the head. On the sides of the board are six cleats by means of which the limbs of the animal can be fastened in any desired position.

With regard to the preservation of the animal, if the dogs are to be kept only a few days, or even a week, the simplest and least injurious method is to leave them on ice in an ice-box when they are not being dissected. A number of dogs can be kept in good condition in this way with but little expense, especially if it is possible to remove the intestines, or at least the large intestine and rectum, after the first day. This method of preserving the animal has the great advantage of not decolorizing any of the tissues, and furthermore prevents the sour odor which soon comes on after using preservative liquids. If it is not possible to make use of this method, and it is necessary to keep the animal for some time, recourse must be had to some of the usual preservative liquids. Immersing the dog in alcohol will keep it from decomposing, but leaves it in such a bad condition for dissecting that it is not to be recommended. Wickerscheimer's liquid injected into the arteries after having previously washed out the blood with 0.6% sol. of NaCl is highly recommended, though my experience with it has been unsatisfactory. The formula for this liquid is as follows: Dissolve in 3 litres of boiling water 100 grms. of alum, 25 grms. of common salt, 12 grms. of potassium nitrate, 60 grms. of potassium carbonate, and 20 grms. of arsenious acid; after cooling add 1½ litres of glycerine and ¼ litre of alcohol. A liquid which I have tried but few times, but which has given satisfaction, is made by mixing one part of glycerine with two parts of a 2% solution of corrosive sublimate, and adding to this mixture crystals of chloral hydrate in the proportion of 2 grms. of chloral to each 100 cc. of the liquid. This liquid keeps the animal pliant, does not destroy the color, and seems to bring out the nerves more distinctly.

Necessary Dissecting Instruments.—Each student should be provided with a small case of dissecting instruments containing at least the following things:

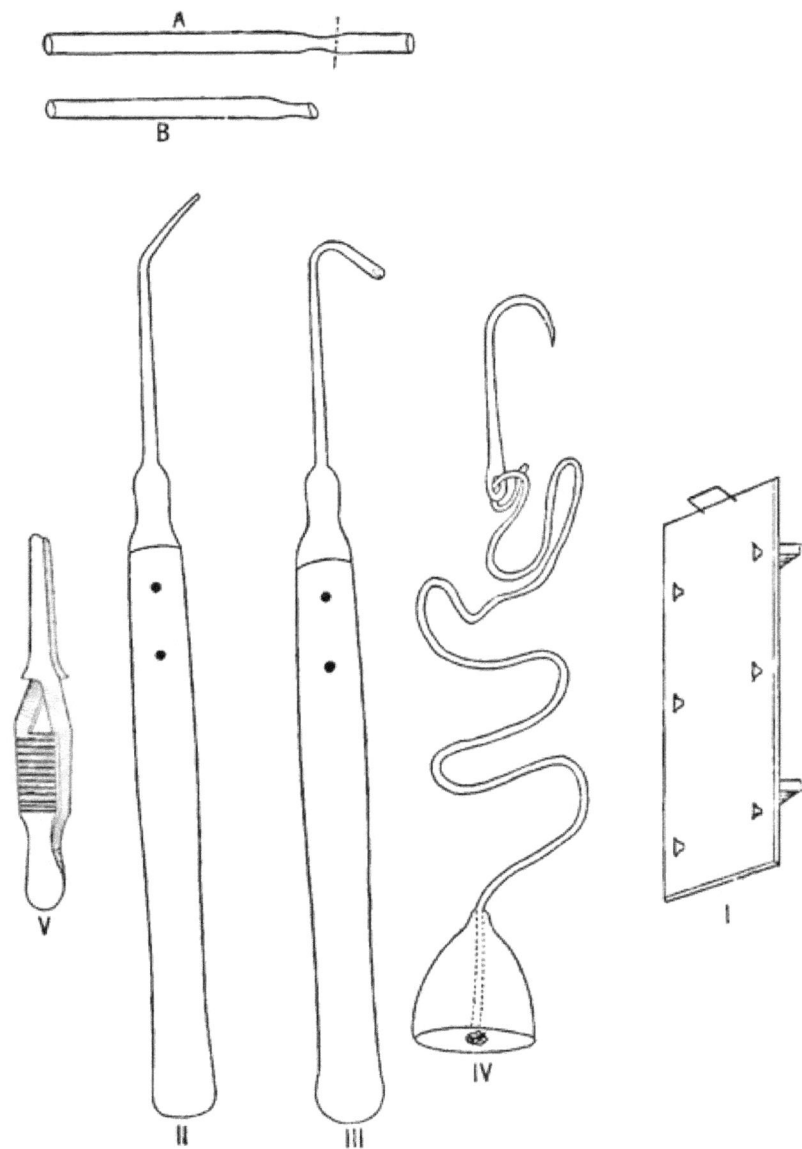

FIG. 1.—INSTRUMENTS.

Two dissecting scalpels, one large and one small.

Two dissecting forceps, one large with blunt ends, and one small with fine points for more delicate work.

Two pairs of scissors, one with large blades for coarse work and one small pair for fine dissection.

One seeker, an instrument of the form shown in II, Fig 1. This will be found very useful in dissecting nerves, blood-vessels, etc., when by careful tearing with the seeker instead of cutting with the scalpel or scissors structures may be revealed which otherwise would be destroyed.

Several weighted hooks of the kind shown in IV, Fig 1. These consist simply of a strong hook to which is attached a cord about two feet in length, carrying at its other end a lead weight. The most convenient weight to use is about 125 grammes, though it is well to have some lighter and some heavier than this. These weighted hooks are useful for holding back the skin, muscles, etc., while dissecting, and are much preferable to the ordinary chain-hooks sold with dissecting cases.

In addition to these instruments there should be at hand for general use several artery-clamps or "serre-fines," either of the form usually sold by instrument makers, or preferably like that shown in V, Fig. 1, having longer and narrower points; several aneurism needles of the form shown in III, Fig. 1, for passing ligature threads round blood-vessels, etc.; one or more pairs of strong bone forceps such as can be obtained from any instrument-maker; a number of small sponges and a small saw.

Cannulas and Injecting Syringe. The cannulas used in injecting can readily be made of any desired size from ordinary glass tubing. The steps in the process are represented in Fig. 1. The glass tubing is first held in the Bunsen flame until softened, and then pulled out gently to the form shown in A. After cooling a scratch is made with a file at the point indicated by the dotted line, the tube broken, and the end ground down obliquely to the form shown in B, upon a grindstone or a piece of ground glass. The narrow neck given to the cannula in this way is necessary in order to hold it firmly when tied in the blood-vessel. The two ends of the cannula should be slightly rounded by heating in the flame. If cannulas are needed for the smaller arteries, for ducts of the salivary gland, etc., the glass tube after being softened in the flame is pulled out to the proper diameter and then this narrowed portion is treated as above.

The requisite features of a good cannula, especially if it is to be used in experiments upon a living animal, are that the neck should be as short as possible, and not any narrower than is necessary to enable the cannula to be tied firmly in the vessel ; and secondly, the lip of the cannula should not be made too oblique, not more so than will facilitate its introduction into the vessel. Three of these cannulas will be required in the injection of the blood-vessels as described in Chapter IV., one for the aorta and two for the venæ cavæ. As these must all be of large size they can easily be made.

With reference to the syringe, the best form undoubtedly is the usual brass injection syringe provided with several brass cannulas and a stop-cock ; it can be obtained from any of the instrument-makers. These syringes, however, are very expensive, and those who cannot afford to buy them will find the common white-metal syringes with double leather piston a cheap and serviceable substitute. These latter can be obtained from Whitall, Tatum & Co. of Philadelphia, of different sizes and at very small cost. The best size to use for the dog is one holding six or eight ounces. Before using this syringe the piston must be left in water for some time to swell, otherwise it will not work tight in the barrel; though if left too long in the water the trouble will be in the other direction. The method of using the syringe in injecting is described in Chapter IV.

CHAPTER I.

MUSCLES OF THE ABDOMEN AND AB
DOMINAL VISCERA.

MUSCLES OF THE ABDOMEN.

Make a median incision through the skin and fat extending from the middle of the sternum to the sym physis pubis ; at the two ends of this make lateral in cisions on each side, and reflect the flaps of skin to gether with the subjacent fat. The muscular portion of the abdominal wall will be exposed.

1. **The Linea Alba** is the white line extending along the ventral mid-line of the abdomen ; it is formed by the fusion of the tendons of the muscles of the two sides.

2. **The External Oblique Muscle** arises by fleshy slips from the posterior ribs, from the fourth to the thirteenth, and in part from the fascia below the thirteenth rib ; the fibres pass obliquely inward and posteriorly, and end in a broad, thin aponeurosis lying along the middle of the abdominal wall and fusing with its fellow of the opposite side.

Make an incision through the aponeurosis at its junction with the muscle fibres, and reflect the muscle outward, separating it carefully from the muscles beneath.

3. **The Internal Oblique Muscle** arises from the crest of the ilium, from Poupart's ligament, and from the aponeurosis of the transversalis muscle anterior to the ilium; its fibres pass obliquely inward and anteriorly to end in a thin aponeurosis which meets its fellow in the mid-line, and lies immediately below that of the external oblique, the two being separated with some difficulty.

4. **The Rectus Abdominis Muscle** is a straight band of fibres arising anteriorly from the sternum and the cartilaginous portions of the posterior ribs, and inserted at the symphysis pubis. Several zigzag lines of fibrous tissue pass transversely across the band of fibres in their course, making it in reality a polygastric muscle.

5. **The Transversalis Abdominis** arises by fleshy slips from the under surface of the posterior ribs and from the region of the lumbar vertebræ; the fibres pass transversely inward, and end in a thin aponeurosis lying beneath the rectus abdominis.

Dissect off very carefully the rectus abdominis and the transversalis; a thin membrane, the peritoneum, *will be exposed covering over the abdominal organs.*

THE ABDOMINAL VISCERA.

After removal of the peritoneum the abdominal viscera are exposed in situ. The intestines are concealed by a special fold of the peritoneum, *the great omentum,* which hangs down from the stomach. The omentum is loaded with fat, and if held up against the light it will be found to be penetrated by a number of minute holes.

A. THE ALIMENTARY CANAL.

1. The Œsophagus. The posterior end of the œsophagus as it enters the stomach can be seen by pressing aside the lobes of the liver; it penetrates the diaphragm below the middle.

2. The Stomach may be studied in situ by lifting up the lobes of the liver so as to expose it fully. When empty it lies obliquely in the body, having a marked bend at the posterior end; when filled it lies more transversely.

a. THE FUNDUS. The left or cardiac end of the stomach is much dilated; the enlarged portion which lies to the left of the entrance of the œsophagus is the fundus.

b. THE GREAT CURVATURE is the line from the fundus along the posterior margin of the stomach to the beginning of the intestines.

c. THE SMALL CURVATURE is the line from the opening of the œsophagus along the anterior margin of the stomach to the beginning of the intestine.

d. THE PYLORUS is the opening of the stomach into the intestines. The position of the pylorus is marked externally by a shallow constriction. This region of the stomach is spoken of as the pyloric end as distinguished from the cardiac end in the neighborhood of the œsophagus.

3. The Intestines.

a. THE DUODENUM is the first portion of the small intestine. It begins at the pylorus, bends suddenly to the posterior for several inches, and then forward again for some distance, making a U-shaped loop, which continues directly into the remainder of the small intestine. The glandular organ lying in the curvature of the duodenum is the pancreas; its attachments must not be disturbed.

b. THE SMALL INTESTINE is several feet in length, and forms a very much convoluted tube which is attached to the dorsal wall of the body by a membrane, the mesentery. Starting from the duodenum, follow the small intestine to its ending in the large intestine.

c. THE MESENTERY is a double layer of the peritoneum which is reflected from the dorsal wall of the abdomen, and encloses the stomach and intestines. Blood-vessels, nerves, and lymphatics pass to the intestines between its two layers.

d. THE CÆCUM is seen at the point where the small intestine passes into the large; it is a coiled diverticulum of the intestine two or more inches in length.

e. THE LARGE INTESTINE commences at the cæcum. The first portion is known as the *colon ;* it passes anteriorly for a short distance as the *ascending colon*, then transversely, the *transverse colon*, and finally posteriorly as the *descending colon*, which is continued directly into

f. THE RECTUM. This is the terminal portion of the large intestine; it lies within the pelvis, and opens to the exterior through the anus.

g. PEYER'S PATCHES. At intervals along the lower portion of the small intestine, on the border opposite the attachment of the mesentery, a number of small oval bodies will be seen, the Peyer's patches. They are masses of lymphoid tissue imbedded in the intestinal wall.

h. LYMPH GLANDS. Enclosed within the layers of the mesentery will be found a number of lymph glands, flattened oval bodies varying in size. Where the cæcum joins the intestine there is a collection of these glands known as the *Pancreas Asselli.*

B. *INTERNAL ANATOMY OF THE ALIMENTARY CANAL AND APPENDICULAR ORGANS.*

Ligature the stomach about one inch to the left of the pylorus, and at the œsophagus. Remove the stomach from the body, cutting through its walls just beyond the ligatures; open it along the great curvature, wash with water and examine.

1. **The Stomach.** The walls of the stomach consist of an outer layer of peritoneum, a middle layer of muscle which is thicker at the pyloric end than elsewhere, and an internal layer of mucous membrane. The last layer is connected to the muscular wall by sub-mucous areolar tissue, and can easily be pulled or dissected away. The mucous membrane is thrown into numerous folds which are especially marked in the cardiac region.

Cut out a piece of the small intestine, selecting a portion which contains one or more Peyer's patches, open along the line of the mesentery, wash thoroughly and examine.

2. **The Small Intestine.** The walls of the small intestine are composed of the same layers as those of the stomach. The mucous membrane is not thrown into folds, but is raised into a number of minute processes which can be seen better with a magnifying-glass. These processes are set closely together like the pile of velvet; they are known as the *Villi.* Examine the appearance of a Peyer's patch when seen from the inside.

3. The Cæcum.

*Cut out the cæcum together with the adjoining por-
tions of the small and large intestine, lay open, and
wash with water.*

The boundary line between the small and the
large intestine is marked by a circular thickening of
the mucous membrane—representing the *ileo-colic
valve*. On one side the mucous membrane of the
small intestine is shaggy with villi; on the other, the
colon, the membrane is smooth. The mucous membrane of the cæcum is thickly studded with small
lymph follicles.

4. The Colon.

The mucous membrane is smooth
throughout, showing no villi, but in some places it is
thrown into irregular folds or rugæ.

5. The Pancreas

lies in the loop of the duo-
denum; it is an elongated glandular body of pinkish
color.

6. The Pancreatic Ducts.

In the dog there are
two main ducts; one, the smaller, opens into the
duodenum about an inch beyond the pylorus, close to
or in connection with the bile duct; the other, larger
duct opens into the duodenum about 1 or 1½ inches
lower down. (The close attachment of the pancreas
to the duodenum conceals these ducts. They can
be demonstrated most easily by tearing away carefully the pancreas from the duodenal wall with a
blunt-pointed instrument, commencing at the pylorus.
The ducts are tougher than the loose connective tissue
attaching the rest of the pancreas, and can be exposed easily in this way.)

7. The Spleen

is an elongated, flattened, dark-
red body lying to the left of the stomach, and connected to it by a fold of the peritoneum, the gastro-

splenic omentum. It is wider at the upper end ; the blood-vessels enter it along the line of attachment of the omentum.

8. The Liver. The anterior surface is convex, and fits against the arched diaphragm to which it is attached by a median fold of peritoneum, the *suspensory ligament.* The organ is relatively large in the dog, and, as in other mammals, may be divided into two principal lobes, the right and the left. Each of these is again subdivided into smaller lobes, the left into two and the right into four, the homologies of which are not properly known. They may be named as follows :

a. THE LEFT CENTRAL LOBE lies against the left half of the diaphragm.

b. THE LEFT LATERAL LOBE, the largest lobe of the liver, lies between the left central and the cardiac end of the stomach.

c. THE RIGHT CENTRAL LOBE lies against the right half of the diaphragm ; it has a deep groove on its under surface for the reception of the gall-bladder.

d. THE RIGHT LATERAL LOBE is just posterior to the right central.

e. THE CAUDATE LOBE, posterior to the last, lies to the right of and dorsal to the pyloric end of the stomach, extending backward to the right kidney.

f. THE SPIGELIAN LOBE, the smallest lobe of the liver, projects into the small curvature of the stomach ; it lies dorsal to a fold of the peritoneum connecting the liver to the stomach, the *hepato-gastric omentum.*

g. THE GALL-BLADDER is a large, thin-walled oval sac imbedded in the right central lobe.

h. THE BILE-DUCT has the arrangement shown in

Fig. 2. It opens into the duodenum about an inch below the pylorus. The duct leading directly from the gall-bladder is known as the *cystic duct*. In the dog it is very short.

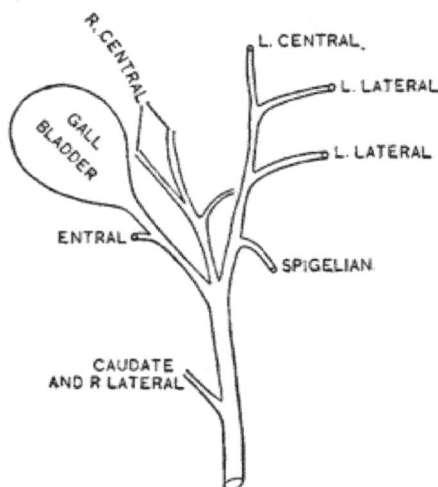

FIG. 2. DIAGRAM OF THE BILE-DUCT AND ITS BRANCHES.

C. THE URINARY SYSTEM.

Remove the liver, spleen, and intestines from the abdomen, taking care not to disturb the reproductive or the urinary organs. In removing the liver it will prove most convenient to double-ligature the large inferior cava above and below the liver, and cut between the ligatures. In removing the intestines double-ligature the rectum as near the anus as possible, and cut between the ligatures.

1. **The Kidneys** are a pair of dark-red oval bodies lying against the dorsal wall of the abdomen, outside of the peritoneum. Each is usually imbedded in fat. If this is carefully removed, the *hilus* will be exposed as a notch on the inner border where the blood-vessels and ureter enter the kidney.

2. **Adrenal Bodies**—one on each side. They lie internal to the upper portion of the kidney, and are surrounded by fat. Each is an elongated, yellowish body about ¾ in. in length.

3. **The Ureter** emerges from the hilus of the kidney, passes backward and inward to reach the under surface of the bladder, into which it opens, well down toward the neck. Make an opening in the ureter about an inch from the bladder, and through this opening pass a bristle or probe into the bladder. Notice that the ureter runs obliquely in the wall of the bladder some distance before it reaches the interior.

4. **The Bladder** is a thin-walled muscular sac which when filled with urine projects some distance above the symphysis pubis.

Cut open the bladder and remove any urine that may be present with a sponge.

Determine the position of the opening of the ureters internally. From each a white thickening of the mucous membrane passes downward to the *urethra*, inclosing a triangular area, the *trigone*.

5. **The Urethra**, the duct of the bladder arises from the lowest portion of the bladder. Its further course will be seen in the dissection of the reproductive system.

6. **The Internal Structure of the Kidneys.**

Remove one from the body and slice it open along its long diameter, preferably a little to one side of the mid-line.

Each kidney has externally a fibrous investment which can be peeled off easily with the forceps. The proper substance of the kidney is divided into a cortical and a medullary layer.

a. THE CORTICAL SUBSTANCE forms the external layer. It is of a darker color, and somewhat mottled owing to the presence of the *Malpighian bodies.*

b. THE MEDULLARY SUBSTANCE forms the internal layer. It is of a lighter color, and striated owing to the peculiar arrangement of the uriniferous tubules and blood-vessels. The uriniferous tubules are united into a number of groups, each of a pyramidal form, and known as the *Malpighian pyramids.* The apices of these pyramids unite to form a ridge lying in the long axis of the kidney. The openings of the uriniferous tubules are found upon this ridge.

c. THE SINUS. The medullary substance encloses a cavity, the sinus, which is a continuation inward of the hilus. It is filled with connective tissue, blood-vessels, and the greatly expanded ureter, which here is known as the *pelvis.* The expanded pelvis clasps the ridge described above, receiving thus the excreted urine. The cavity of the pelvis also extends outward for some distance along each pyramid.

D.   THE DIAPHRAGM.

The diaphragm is the muscular septum between the abdomen and the thorax, and can now be examined from the abdominal side. It is a dome-shaped partition, partly muscular, partly membranous.

1. **The Central Tendon** lies at the top of the dome. It is a thin membrane passing into muscular substance at all points of its circumference.

2. **The Muscular Substance** has three origins :

a. Posteriorly from the bodies of several of **the** lumbar vertebræ by two thick muscular slips or crura.

b. From the ensiform cartilage.

c. From the cartilages of the posterior ribs,

From these points the muscular substance passes up along the walls of the thorax for some distance, and then bends inward somewhat abruptly to end in the central tendon.

E. FEMALE REPRODUCTIVE ORGANS.

If dissected upon a new dog, open the abdomen as in the dissection of the abdominal viscera, and remove the stomach, intestines and liver. Then cut through the skin and muscles above the pubis symphysis so as to expose this and the rami running from it above and below for a short distance. Cut through the symphysis with bone forceps, and the rami above and below the obturator foramen at a distance of about one-half inch on each side of the symphysis. Remove carefully the pieces of bone thus isolated.

1. **The Ovaries.** A pair of oval bodies of a pale color, lying posterior and dorsal to the kidneys, at the termination of the oviducts. Each, in the small dogs, is less than one one-half inch long, and is concealed in a membranous capsule, which must be cut open to fully expose the ovary.

2. **The Oviducts.** Each consists of two parts : posteriorly a thick-walled tube, which unites with its fellow of the opposite side to form the body of the uterus ; anteriorly a very small convoluted tube lying close to the ovary—the Fallopian tube. The oviduct is connected to the dorsal wall of the abdomen throughout its whole length by a broad fold of peritoneum, *the broad ligament.*

a. THE FALLOPIAN TUBE is very narrow and slightly convoluted. It lies close to the ovary ; its anterior end expands into a capsule surrounding the ovary and communicating with the abdominal cavity by a small opening; its posterior end suddenly expands into a horn of the uterus.

b. The Uterus consists of two horns, each beginning from the posterior end of the Fallopian tube, and a *body* formed by the fusion of the posterior portions of the horns. The body of the uterus is directly continuous with the vagina.

3. **The Vagina** is quite wide, and passes directly to the posterior to end in the vestibule or urino-genital canal.

4. **The Urethra.** Immediately ventral to the vagina lie the bladder and urethra. The latter runs along the ventral wall of the vagina, and finally the two unite within the pelvis to form the vestibule or urino-genital canal.

5. **The Vestibule** formed as stated above, lies ventral to the rectum, and opens to the exterior. It has very vascular walls.

Lay open the vestibule carefully, beginning at the exterior, and cutting along the dorsal mid-line.

6. **The Clitoris**, a small organ homologous with the penis of the male, is found just within the vestibule on its ventral wall. It possesses essentially the same structure as the penis, though on a smaller scale. It has a glans clitoridis and two corpora cavernosa connected with the ischia.

7. Note the connection of the urethra and vagina with the vestibule.

If dissected upon a new dog, open the abdomen as in the dissection of the abdominal viscera. Remove the stomach, liver and intestines without disturbing the urinary or reproductive organs.

1. **The Scrotal Sac** is a pouch-like diverticulum of the skin of the abdomen lying posterior to the symphysis pubis. It contains the testes.

2. **The Testes.** Dissect the skin from the scrotal sac and the proximal half of the penis; the two testes will be exposed. Each is enclosed in a thin sheath of peritoneum, the *tunica vaginalis.* Within this lies a firm white sheath of connective tissue, the *tunica albuginea*, forming the proper capsule of the organ. At the anterior end of each testis is the *spermatic cord* enclosed in its sheath, and consisting of the spermatic artery and vein and the vas deferens bound into one cord. It may be followed forward to the abdominal wall which it penetrates through an oblique opening, the *inguinal canal.* Along the dorsal side of the spermatic cord is a thin band of muscle fibres, the *cremaster muscle;* it arises from Poupart's ligament at the symphysis and passes to the testes, over which its fibres spread.

Slit open the tunic of the testis and spermatic cord.

The testis will be fully exposed as an oval pinkish body about an inch long (in small dogs), and suspended by the spermatic cord.

3. **The Epididymis** is an irregular convoluted mass lying along the inner and dorsal border of the testis. It is divisible into several portions.

a. THE CAPUT EPIDIDYMIS is the enlarged portion lying in contact with the anterior end of the testis.

b. THE CAUDA EPIDIDYMIS forms the posterior narrower portion. It is connected with the testis by a short ligament, the *gubernaculum*.

4. **The Vas Deferens**—the narrow tube forming the continuation of the cauda epididymis. It passes along the spermatic cord, enters the abdomen, and finally opens into the urethra—as will be seen in the later dissection.

5. **The Spermatic Artery and Vein,** found also in the spermatic cord. They supply the testis with blood.

Cut through the pubis as directed in the dissection of the female organs. Ligature the rectum, and remove it if not done in the previous dissection. Clear away the fat, etc., from the neck of the bladder to the root of the penis.

6. **The Vas Deferens.** After passing through the inguinal canal it turns inward to the dorsal surface of the neck of the bladder lying internal to the ureter. The two vasa deferentia open close together into the dorsal surface of the urethra a short distance beyond its origin from the bladder.

7. **The Prostate Gland** is a large glandular mass encircling the urethra at the same point. Its ducts open into the floor of the urethra.

8. **The Urethra** after leaving the prostate gland continues under the symphysis pubis to reach the penis. This portion is known as the urino-genital canal, and has very vascular walls.

9. **Cowper's Glands** are very small in the dog. Each opens into the urino-genital canal by a small duct as it passes under the symphysis.

10. **The Penis.** At its root the lower aspect is

formed by the *corpus spongiosum*, in the middle of which lies the urethra. The sides and upper surface are formed by the two *corpora cavernosa*, white tough bodies which are very vascular, and are attached to the ischial bones. At the distal end of the penis these bodies end in the long thick *glans penis*, which forms the terminal portion of the corpus spongiosum. A cross-section through the penis will give a good view of the arrangement of the three corpora of which it is composed.

11. **The Os Penis.** In the glans penis and for a short distance between the corpora cavernosa is found the large penis bone. It lies over the urethra, and is grooved on the under side.

12. **The Prepuce.** The end of the glans penis is covered by a movable fold of the integument, the prepuce.

CHAPTER II.

MUSCLES OF THE SHOULDER AND ARM.

MUSCLES OF THE SHOULDER.

Dissect off the skin together with the underlying skin muscles from the neck, shoulder and arm. Begin to dissect from the dorsal side, placing the animal upon its right or left side.

1. **The Trapezius Muscle** arises from the occipital bone, and from the dorsal mid-line above the spinous processes of the cervical and anterior thoracic vertebræ. From this extensive line of origin the fibres converge toward the scapula and humerus. Carefully cleaning the muscle from fat, fascia, etc., it will be found to be composed of three divisions.

a. The Anterior Trapezius is the most anterior division; it arises from the occipital bone, and from the dorsal mid-line of the neck above the spinous processes of all but the last cervical vertebræ. The muscular fibres converge toward the humerus, where they fuse with a long muscle, the levator humeri, and are inserted with it into the lower part of the shaft of the humerus.

b. The Middle Trapezius arises from the dorsal mid-line above the spinous processes of the posterior cervical and anterior thoracic vertebræ in a continuous line with the insertion of the anterior trapezius. Its fibres pass to the spine of the scapula, and are inserted along the greater portion of its anterior edge. There is usually a space between this and the anterior division near the origin of the fibres, which is filled up with fat, connective tissue, lymphatic glands, etc.

c. THE POSTERIOR TRAPEZIUS arises above the spinous processes of the anterior thoracic vertebræ in a continuous line with the middle trapezius. The fibres pass obliquely forward to be inserted along the posterior edge of the outer or vertebral portion of the spine of the scapula.

In man these three divisions are more completely united to form a single trapezius muscle.

Cut the three divisions of the trapezius at their insertions and reflect the cut ends dorsally to their origins. The following muscles will be exposed.

2. The Rhomboideus Minor. It arises from the dorsal mid-line above the spinous processes of the posterior cervical vertebræ, just beneath the origin of the trapezius. The fibres pass obliquely to the scapula and are inserted into the anterior angle of the vertebral margin.

a. THE OCCIPITO SCAPULARIS. Lying along the inner margin of the rhomboideus minor is a narrow band of muscle, the occipito scapularis, which arises from the occipital bone and is inserted into the scapula along with the rhomboideus, the two forming one muscle at the insertion. This muscle is known also as the rhomboideus capitis or rhomboideus occipitalis in human anatomy.

3. The Rhomboideus Major arises from the spinous processes of the four or five most anterior thoracic vertebræ—its origin being in a continuous line with that of the rhomboideus minor, from which indeed it is not separate in the dog. The fibres pass straight to the scapula, to be inserted along the vertebral edge.

4. The **Levator Anguli Scapulæ** arises from the transverse processes of the posterior cervical vertebræ. The fibres form a broad sheet of muscle, and are inserted into the under or ventral side of the scapula near the anterior angle of the vertebral margin. Its insertion is just to the inside of that of the rhomboideus minor.

5. The **Levator Scapulæ** is a narrow flat band of muscle which has its origin from the transverse process of the atlas, and is inserted into the acromion process of the scapula and a small extent of the neighboring portion of the spine. Its insertion is just to the inner side of that of the middle trapezius. This muscle corresponds to the *levator claviculæ* of the cat.

6. The **Levator Humeri** is a muscle similar in shape to the last, lying nearer to the ventral mid-line. It arises from the skull posterior to the external auditory meatus, and is inserted below the middle of the humerus, on its ventral face. Just before the muscle passes over the shoulder-joint it is intersected by a transverse line of tendon dividing it into two portions, the anterior of which corresponds to the clavo-mastoid of the cat, while the posterior division represents the clavo-deltoid.

7. The **Sterno-mastoid** lies to the inner side of the last-mentioned muscle ; it will be described in connection with the dissection of the neck.

8. The **Supra-spinatus** is a large muscle occupying the whole of the supra-spinous fossa, from which its fibres originate. They pass outward to be inserted into the great tubercle of the humerus.

9. **The Deltoid Muscle.** In the dog it is divided into two separate muscles, not including the portion of the levator humeri which corresponds to the clavo-deltoid.

a. The acromio-deltoid, the smaller division, takes its origin from the acromion process, and is inserted into a ridge along the outer surface of the proximal third of the humerus.

b. The spino-deltoid arises by a strong fascia from the posterior border of the spine of the scapula along most of its extent, and is inserted into the humerus together with the acromio-deltoid.

Cut through the bellies of the deltoid muscles, and reflect the cut ends.

10. **The Infra-spinatus Muscle** fills up the infra-spinous fossa from which it arises. Its fibres end in a strong tendon which is inserted into the great tuberosity of the humerus just below the insertion of the supra-spinatus.

11. **The Teres Minor** is seen just posterior to the infra-spinatus near its insertion. When dissected out it will be found to arise along the posterior margin of the scapula by a tendinous expansion lying beneath the infra-spinatus. It is inserted into the humerus below the great tuberosity.

12. **The Latissimus Dorsi** is a very large muscle arising by a fascia from the spinous processes of the lumbar and posteroir thoracic vertebrae. From this origin the fibres form a wide sheet of muscle lying on the dorso-lateral wall of the thorax, and converge anteriorly toward the humerus. It ends in a tendinous expansion which fuses with the sheath of the triceps medius and teres major, through which its action on the humerus takes place. Just before its insertion the

latissimus gives off a muscular slip, which passes along
the arm, superficial to the triceps, to be inserted into
the olecranon process of the ulna. It might be called
the *latissimus extensor muscle.*

*Cut through the latissimus dorsi at its insertion.
Cut across also the pectoralis group of muscles and the
loose connective tissue, nerves, blood-vessels, etc., which
bind the arm to the side of the thorax. The scapula
will then fall outward, displaying the following muscles.*

13. **The Teres Major**—the muscular band lying
along the posterior margin of the scapula. It is inserted by a flat tendon into the upper part of the
humerus, between the biceps and coraco-brachialis
muscles.

14. **The Sub-scapular Muscle** is the large mass of
muscle filling up the sub-scapular fossa. It has three
or four tendinous lines separating the muscle incompletely into fasciculi. The fibres converge toward the head of the humerus, into which they are
inserted, the tendon passing through the capsular
ligament of the shoulder-joint. At the anterior
margin of the scapula the sub-scapular muscle fuses
more or less with the supra-spinatus.

15. **The Serratus Magnus** is the large muscle connecting the vertebral margin of the scapula to the
wall of the thorax. Anteriorly it fuses with the levator anguli scapuli, the two constituting in this animal
in reality but one muscle. The portion which arises
from the transverse processes of the cervical vertebræ
may be called the levator anguli scapuli, while the
portion arising from the ribs is the serratus magnus.
It springs from the first eight ribs by fleshy slips, and
is inserted along the vertebral margin of the scapula.

MUSCLES OF THE ARM.

16. The Biceps Muscle lies on the inner and ventral face of the humerus. Its anterior end is covered over by the insertion of the pectoralis muscles upon the humerus. The biceps arises by a single strong tendon from the edge of the glenoid fossa (coracoid process), the tendon passing through the capsular ligament of the joint. The muscle is inserted by a strong tendon chiefly into the ulna, though it is attached also to the radius by a smaller slip.

17. The Coraco-brachialis is a small muscle lying to the inner side of the proximal end of the biceps. It arises by a single tendon from the coracoid process, passes over the head of the humerus, and is inserted into the inner side of the humerus just beneath the tendon of the teres major.

18. The Triceps Brachialis is the large mass of muscle lying along the dorsal aspect of the humerus. It serves to extend the forearm. In the dog it has four divisions.

a. The largest division is an irregular muscle, formed apparently by the fusion of two muscles; it arises along the posterior margin of the scapula, the attachment being especially strong near the glenoid fossa, and is inserted into the olecranon process of the ulna. The other three divisions lie between this one and the humerus, and agree pretty well in position with the three heads of the triceps in man.

b. The most internal of these three divisions arises from the humerus at the insertion of the coraco-brachialis, and also by a line of fascia along the middle third of the humerus.

c. The most external of the three divisions arises from the head of the humerus just beneath the insertion of the teres minor, and from fascia along the outer part of the humerus.

d. The middle division arises, in common with the last, just beyond the head of the humerus.

The divisions *b, c* and *d* are inserted into the olecranon process along with *a*.

Cut through the bellies of the triceps, and reflect the cut ends.

19. **The Brachialis Anticus** is a flat muscle closely adherent to the humerus ; it arises from the dorsal and external aspect of the humerus throughout most of its extent. The fibres pass over to the anterior or ventral face of the humerus, and at the elbow end in a tendon which is inserted into the ulna. The tendon passes between the two terminal tendons of the biceps, fusing with them.

20. **The Sub-anconeus** is a very small muscle which arises from the dorsal surface of the distal end of the humerus round the margins of the olecranon fossa. The muscle adheres closely to the humerus, and is inserted into the olecranon process and outer side of the ulna.

CHAPTER III.

THE THORACIC VISCERA, BUCCAL CAVITY, PHARYNX AND LARYNX.

THE THORACIC VISCERA.

Dissect off the skin and muscles from the thorax. With the bone forceps cut carefully through all the bony ribs at a distance of several inches on each side of the sternum. Remove the triangular piece of the thoracic wall thus isolated.

A. In removing this piece notice the vertical fold of serous membrane passing from the heart to the sternum ; it is a portion of the pleural membrane known as the *anterior mediastinum.*

1. **The Thymus Gland** lies in the anterior part of the thorax anterior to the heart. It varies in size with the age of the animal, being larger in the young and decreasing in size as the animal grows older.

2. **The Lungs** will be found collapsed when the thorax is opened ; in the closed thorax they filled all the space not occupied by the heart, great blood-vessels, etc. They lie quite free in the cavity, except at the roots, i.e., where the blood-vessels and bronchi enter them.

The left lung is divided into two lobes, the upper of which is incompletely subdivided by a deep notch.

The right lung is divided into four lobes. The most posterior of these, the *infra-cardiac* lobe, projects between the heart and the diaphragm, enclosed in a special fold of the right pleura.

3. **The Pleuræ.** Each side of the thorax is lined by a delicate membrane, the *parietal pleura*, which at the anterior end of the thorax bends backward along the great blood-vessels to the root of the lungs, and thence is reflected over the external surface of the lungs, forming the *visceral pleura*. In the unopened thorax the lungs fill the whole cavity, and the parietal and visceral layers of the pleura come into contact, forming a smooth sliding-surface for the expansion and collapse of the lungs. The right and left pleural sacs meet in the mid-line to form a double-walled septum, the *mediastinum*. The portion of this extending from the heart to the sternum is the *anterior mediastinum*. The portion between the dorsal surface of the heart and the vertebral column is the *posterior mediastinum*, it encloses between its layers the œsophagus, the descending aorta, the lower portion of the trachea, etc.

4. **The Phrenic Nerves,** one on each side, lying between the heart and the lung. Follow each to its termination in the diaphragm.

5. **The Trachea** can be seen passing into the thorax from the neck. Its further dissection should be made after that of the heart.

6. **The Œsophagus** is a wide muscular tube lying along the dorsal wall of the thorax. It is easily seen by lifting up the right lung.

B. DISSECTION OF THE HEART AND GREAT BLOOD-VESSELS OF THE THORAX.

1. The Pericardium is the membranous sac in which the heart is enclosed. Like the pleura and the peritoneum it is a double-walled sac. One layer, the visceral, is attached closely to the muscular substance of the heart ; the other, the parietal, lies loosely round the heart. The two layers meet at the roots of the great blood-vessels, and hold between them a little serous liquid, the pericardial liquid. Notice the attachment of the pericardium, the parietal layer, to the diaphragm.

Cut away the pericardium, and clean as carefully as possible the roots of the large veins and arteries arising from the heart.

The greater portion of the surface of the heart facing ventrally is made up of the right ventricle. Anterior and to the right lies the right auricle. The tip of the heart—the apex—is formed by the left ventricle alone. The left ventricle makes up also the greater portion of the dorsal surface of the heart. The position of the internal septum between the two ventricles is marked externally by a groove, containing a coronary artery and vein, which begins down toward the apex on the ventral surface, and runs obliquely around to the dorsal side.

Determine the positions of the right and left ventricles, and the right and left auricles. Each of the auricles consists of a main cavity, the *atrium*, into which the veins open, and an *auricular appendix*, usually the most conspicuous portion of the auricle.

1. **The Veins opening into the Right Auricle**.

a. THE SUPERIOR VENA CAVA (præ-cava) opens into the anterior end of the auricle, and brings back venous blood from the head, neck, upper limbs and thorax.

b. Just above the root of the right lung the superior cava receives the large *azygos* vein. Lift up the right lung and follow the azygos along the dorsal wall of the thorax to the diaphragm. Notice the side branches, the intercostal veins, which it receives from the walls of the thorax.

c. THE INFERIOR VENA CAVA (post-cava) empties into the posterior end of the auricle. Follow it to the diaphragm.

2. **Arteries arising from the Right Ventricle**.

a. THE PULMONARY ARTERY arises from the anterior and dorsal corner of the ventricle, passes dorsally for a short distance, and then divides into the right and left pulmonary arteries which go to the two lungs, entering each at its root. They carry venous blood from the heart to the lungs.

3. **Veins opening into the Left Auricle**.

a. THE PULMONARY VEINS. There are two principal veins on each side : on the left side, one from each lobe ; on the right side, one from the two upper and one from the two lower lobes. These four veins converge to enter the auricle, the two from the right lung passing directly underneath the right auricle to reach their destination. These veins bring back arterial blood from the lungs to the heart.

4. **Arteries arising from the Left Ventricle**.

a. THE AORTA arises from the anterior end of the ventricle, immediately dorsal to the origin of the pulmonary artery. It passes for a short distance anteriorly, the *ascending aorta*, then curves posteriorly and dorsally, forming the *arch of the aorta*, from which the arteries for the head, upper limbs, etc., are given off, and finally passes posteriorly along the dorsal wall of the thorax, the *descending aorta*, lying dorsal to the œsophagus.

This portion gives off side branches—the *intercostal arteries*—to the ribs, during its course in the thorax.

5. The Ductus Arteriosus may be found as a ligament connecting the pulmonary artery, just before its division into right and left pulmonary arteries, with the aorta. In embryonic life it is a vessel forming a communication between these two vessels, and in adult life is occasionally found patent. It is a remnant of the connection between the fourth and fifth arterial arches of the embryo.

C. THE INTERNAL ANATOMY OF THE HEART.

Cut across the great vessels about half an inch from the heart, and remove the heart from the body.

1. The Auricles.

Cut away the outer wall of both auricles and wash out the contained blood.

a. THE RIGHT AURICLE. The wall of the auricle is thin ; that of the appendix is thicker and marked internally by muscular ridges, as is also the wall of the auricle in part.

b. THE SEPTUM AURICULARUM is the thin partition between the two auricles. An oval depression in it is known as the *fossa ovalis ;* it marks the position of the fœtal *foramen ovale.* If the dog is young this may still be found open.

c. THE CORONARY VEIN. The opening of this vein into the auricle is seen just posterior to the opening of the inferior cava, lying between it and the opening of the auricle into the ventricle. Follow its course back along the groove between the auricle and the ventricle.

d. The Auriculo-ventricular Orifice. The crescentic opening leading into the right ventricle.

e. The Left Auricle has thin walls like the right. The walls of the appendix are thicker and marked internally by muscular ridges.

f. The Left Auriculo-ventricular Orifice. The circular opening leading into the left ventricle.

2. The Ventricles.

Cut across the two ventricles at some distance from the apex—in the lower third of the right ventricle.

The cavity of the right ventricle has a crescentic shape ; the wall is relatively thin. The cavity of the left ventricle is circular ; its walls are quite thick. The ventricular septum is very thick and arched, with the convexity projecting into the cavity of the right ventricle. The cavity of the left ventricle extends into the apex, while that of the right ventricle terminates some distance anterior to it.

Remove the auricles close to the base of the ventricles, and cut short the aorta and pulmonary artery. A good view of the relative positions of the four openings into the ventricles is thus obtained.

a. The Tricuspid Valve of the right ventricle. It guards the right auriculo-ventricular orifice, and is formed by three membranous flaps attached round the margin of the orifice. The free borders project into the ventricle, and are connected to its wall by tendinous cords, the *chordæ tendineæ*, which end in papillary elevations of the ventricular wall known as the *papillary muscles*. Some of the chordæ tendineæ go to two flaps, or one flap may have chordæ from two papillary muscles.

Cut through the right ventricular wall between two of the flaps to get a better view of their attachments. Note the reticulated structure of the ventricular walls—the **columnæ carneæ**.

b. THE PULMONARY ARTERY. The portion of the right ventricular cavity leading into the pulmonary artery is known as the *conus arteriosus* and forms a funnel-like recess. The opening into the artery is guarded by three pocket-valves, the *semi-lunar valves*, which can be exposed easily with a probe from the opening of the artery above. Cut through the conus and artery longitudinally to get a better view of the valves.

c. THE MITRAL VALVE of the left ventricle guards the left auriculo-ventricular orifice. It resembles the tricuspid, with the exception that there are only two flaps or cusps.

d. THE AORTIC SEMI-LUNAR VALVES, three in number, have the same structure as those of the pulmonary artery.

e. THE CORONARY ARTERIES. Behind two of the aortic semi-lunar valves will be found the openings of the two coronary arteries arising from the base of the aorta. Run a probe into each and follow its course for some distance.

3. **The Trachea and Bronchi.** Find the trachea as it enters the thorax. Dissect it toward the lungs. It divides into two large branches, the bronchi, one for each lung. If one of the bronchi is followed into the lung to which it is distributed it will be found to give off smaller bronchi at intervals, and these in turn give off still smaller branches, the whole system forming

what is known as the *bronchial tree.* The terminal twigs of this system end in the air-sacs or alveoli, little membranous bags, in the walls of which the capillaries of the pulmonary artery are distributed.

D. DISSECTION OF THE BUCCAL CAVITY.

Remove the skin from the head. Lay open the mouth on one side by cutting through the cheek with a pair of scissors, and continuing the cut backward across the bone with bone forceps or saw.

1. **The Roof of the Mouth.**

a. THE HARD PALATE, formed by the palatine processes of the maxillary and palatine bones.   It is covered by pigmented mucous membrane which is raised into a number of transverse ridges.   The soft palate is continued backward from this and ends in a free notched border.

b. THE TONSILS are two pinkish-gray eminences lying lateral to the soft palate and above the root of the tongue.

c. THE TEETH.   Verify the dental formula i. $\frac{3}{3}$, c. $\frac{1}{1}$, pm. $\frac{4}{4}$, m. $\frac{2}{3}$.

2. **The Floor of the Mouth.**

a. THE TONGUE is attached along the greater part of its length to the floor of the mouth.   The mucous membrane covering the upper surface shows three different kinds of papillæ: the *circumvallate,* four in number, arranged along two converging lines at the root of the tongue; the *fungiform,* found generally over the dorsal surface and especially thick at the tip; the *filiform,* which toward the root are larger than in front, and end in free notched borders. They are thickly scattered over the whole dorsal surface.

3. **The Pharynx** is the continuation backward of the buccal cavity beyond the soft palate. The nasal cavity also opens into it above the palate. To expose it better the symphysis of the mandibles may be cut through, allowing one side of the lower jaw to be depressed.

a. THE EPIGLOTTIS is the conspicuous V-shaped lobe of cartilage projecting into the pharynx.

b. THE GLOTTIS, or RIMA GLOTTIDIS. Posteriorly the pharynx ends in two openings. One of these is slit-like and placed ventrally ; the inconspicuous folds bounding it are the *false vocal cords*, while immediately below or posterior to these are two more distinct folds, the *true vocal cords*. The slit between the true cords is the glottis ; it leads into the larynx. The epiglottis projects over this opening and covers it during the act of swallowing.

c. THE ŒSOPHAGUS. The second opening at the posterior of the pharynx is the beginning of the œsophagus. It lies dorsal to the glottis.

d. THE EUSTACHIAN TUBES. Slit open the soft palate. The openings of the Eustachian tubes will be seen in the anterior portion of the dorsal wall of the pharynx, on a level with the nasal cavity.

To expose the nasal cavity insert the blade of the scissors into the anterior nares of one side and cut back close to the septum, using the bone forceps if necessary. Remove also the external wall of this side of the nasal cavity. The structure of this side is destroyed, but now by carefully removing as much of the septum as possible the nasal chamber of the other side will be exposed.

4. **The Nasal Cavity.** Note the arrangement of the turbinate bones. The respiratory passage lies

between the lower turbinate and the palate, while the olfactory passages proper lie between the upper ethmoidal turbinates.

a. THE SCHNEIDERIAN MEMBRANE is the mucous membrane covering the upper turbinates. It is usually of a darker color than the rest of the nasal mucous membrane, and contains the end organs or cells of the olfactory nerve-fibres.

5. The Salivary Glands.

Dissect on the side not previously used.   No especial directions are required.

a. THE PAROTID GLAND is not very prominent in the dog. It lies posterior to and somewhat in front of the ear, and forms a somewhat indefinite pinkish mass.

b. STENSON'S DUCT, the duct of the parotid, arises from the ventral margin of the gland, runs across the middle of the masseter muscle, bends inward at the border of the muscle, and opens into the mouth by a small aperture on the inside of the cheek opposite the posterior portion of the last premolar of the maxilla. Insert a probe into the duct and demonstrate the opening into the mouth.

c. THE SUB-MAXILLARY GLAND forms on each side a compact mass lying just posterior to the angle of the mandible and concealed by connective tissue, which must be cleared away.

d. WHARTON'S DUCT. The duct of the sub-maxilliary will be exposed best if the attachment of the digastric (see page 65) to the mandible is cut, and this muscle reflected backward as far as possible. If the thin sheet of muscle (mylo-hyoid) lying in the floor of the mouth is now carefully cut the duct will be exposed, and can be traced back to the gland and forward to its opening upon the floor of the mouth.

e. THE CHORDA TYMPANI, the nerve of the sub-maxillary, is also shown in this dissection. Coming out from underneath the mandible and passing toward the ventral mid-line will be seen the large *lingual nerve.* Just at the point it comes into view it gives off a minute branch, the chorda, which runs

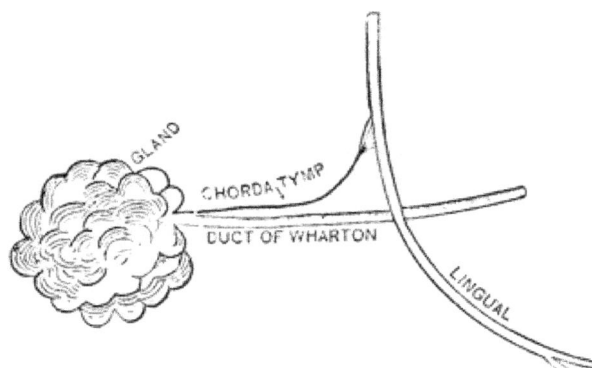

FIG. 3.—DIAGRAM OF THE SUB-MAXILLARY GLAND.

to the duct and thence to the gland. The relations of these parts is shown in Fig. 3.

f. THE SUB-LINGUAL GLAND lies along the outer side of the duct of Wharton, and is crossed by the lingual nerve. It is a small narrow glandular body which opens upon the floor of the mouth by several small ducts.

6. The Larynx. Remove the larynx and the hyoid bone with its processes from the body for more careful examination. The larynx consists of four principal cartilages. *a.* The *thyroid*, the largest and most anterior; the sides or wings are widely open behind. *b.* The *cricoid*, having somewhat the shape of a seal ring, being narrow on the ventral surface and expanded dorsally. It is connected to the thyroid by ligaments and muscles. *c.* The *arytenoid* cartilages are two small triangular cartilages attached to the anterior end of the dorsal side of the cricoid.   The vocal cords are connected with these cartilages.

7. **The Hyoid Bone** consists of the body or basi-hyal connected with the thyroid, the two long anterior cornua, each composed of three pieces, the cerato-hyal united with the basi-hyal, the epi-hyal and the stylo-hyal, the last being connected with the base of the skull by a flexible cartilage, and the two shorter posterior horns each composed of a single bone, the thyro-hyal, which unites with the lateral portion of the thyroid.

CHATER IV.

DISSECTION OF THE VASCULAR SYSTEM.

INJECTION. *In dissecting the blood-vessels it will be found most convenient to inject the arteries and veins with different colors, using coarse injection, which will not pass beyond the capillaries. The injection material recommended is plaster of Paris. The dry powder should be mixed with water, stirring all the time, until the liquid has the consistency of a very thin paste ; the coloring matter is then added. This mixture should not be made until it is ready to be used, since it sets quickly. For the veins the best coloring matter to use is a saturated aqueous solution of Prussian blue ; for the arteries, freshly prepared chromate of lead held in suspension in water. To prepare this latter make a 1% solution of ammonium or potassium bichromate and a strong solution of acetate of lead. add the latter solution to the former, stirring all the while, until the bichromate solution is all precipitated as yellow chromate of lead. Allow the liquid to stand until the precipitate settles to the bottom, then decant the supernatant liquid. Wash the precipitate several times with water, de-*

canting the excess, and finally mix the chromate held
in suspension in a little water with the plaster-of-Paris
solution.

The injection of the vessels is best done as follows:
Dissect off the skin and muscles from the ventral surface of the thorax. Open the thorax by cutting
through the cartilaginous ribs at their junction with
the bony ribs on each side of the sternum from above
the diaphragm to the third rib, then cut transversely
across the sternum and remove the piece of thorax
thus isolated. On the under side of the piece of the
sternum left at the anterior end of the thorax run the
two sternal arteries and veins; these must be ligated
either by dissecting them out and tying each separately,
or by passing a thread round the piece of sternum
and binding firmly.

Take a large cannula, to which a bit of rubber tubing is attached, fill it with 0.6% solution of NaCl,
clamp the tubing, and then insert the cannula
into the aorta where it springs from the heart and
ligature it firmly. Fill the syringe with the 0.6% solution
of NaCl and inject it into the aorta, making mean-
while a cut in the right auricle through which the blood
can escape. Continue the injection of NaCl solution
until all the blood is washed out. Then make the
yellow mixture of plaster of Paris and inject it until
the arteries are thoroughly filled. If any escape takes
place from the small arteries cut in opening the thorax,
these arteries can easily be ligated. In this as in all other
injections care must be taken not to let air get into
the vessel. The rubber tubing on the cannula should be
clamped each time the syringe is removed to be filled;
while in filling the syringe one must be careful also
to remove all air by holding it in an inverted position

after it is filled, and pushing up the piston-rod until the injection flows from the end.

To inject the veins it will be more convenient to inject the superior cava and inferior cava separately. Introduce a cannula filled with the blue injection into each, and then force in the injection as in the arteries until the veins are well filled. A sponge should be at hand during the whole process to sop up any liquid or injection material which may escape into the thoracic cavity. By this process of injection the heart is not left in good condition for dissecting, but this is supposed to have been done before.

The injection of the arteries and veins can be made also from the femoral artery and vein of one of the legs, injecting in each case toward the heart and first washing out the blood with salt solution. This method, however, is not so likely, in inexperienced hands at least, to give good results. After injecting the animal must be left some little time before using to allow the plaster to set.

A. THE DESCENDING AORTA.

Find the aorta just beyond the arch, and dissect toward the posterior. Turn the heart and lungs toward the right, dissecting along the left side of the thorax. If necessary cut off the ribs on this side nearer to the vertebral column.

1. **The Intercostal Arteries** come off from the aorta in pairs in the spaces between the ribs ; they pass outward along the lower or posterior margins of the ribs. The first intercostal from the aorta supplies the 5th or sometimes the 4th rib, giving a branch to the rib above. The 1st, 2d and 3d ribs are supplied by the superior intercostal artery (see below).

2. **The Bronchial Arteries** arise either from the 3d

aortic intercostal or from the aorta at that level, pass beneath the œsophagus to reach the root of the lungs, and thence penetrate the lungs, following the bronchi.

3. **The Cœliac Axis** is a large branch given off from the aorta as it pierces the diaphragm ; it passes for a short distance into the abdominal cavity, and then divides into three branches, as follows :

a. THE HEPATIC ARTERY, the most anterior branch, passes beneath the œsophagus at its junction with the stomach, sends one or two large branches to the liver, the true hepatic artery, one branch to the duodenum, and finally is distributed to the pancreas.

b. THE CORONARY ARTERY, the smallest of the three branches, is distributed chiefly along the small curvature of the stomach.

c. THE SPLENIC ARTERY, the most posterior division, splits into two main branches distributed chiefly to the spleen. Each sends branches to the stomach along the great curvature, and some smaller branches are given off to the pancreas also.

4. **The Superior Mesenteric Artery** arises from the aorta a short distance posterior to the cœliac axis. It gives off a number of branches which supply the small intestine and the greater portion of the large intestine. Follow its course in the mesentery.

5. Posterior to the last two small arteries are given off, that on the left side being somewhat anterior to the other. Each divides into two branches, one of which passes anteriorly, the *phrenic artery*, to supply the diaphragm, while the other is distributed to the muscles of the abdominal wall. This latter branch supplies also the adrenal bodies.

6. **The Renal Arteries** are two large trunks, one on

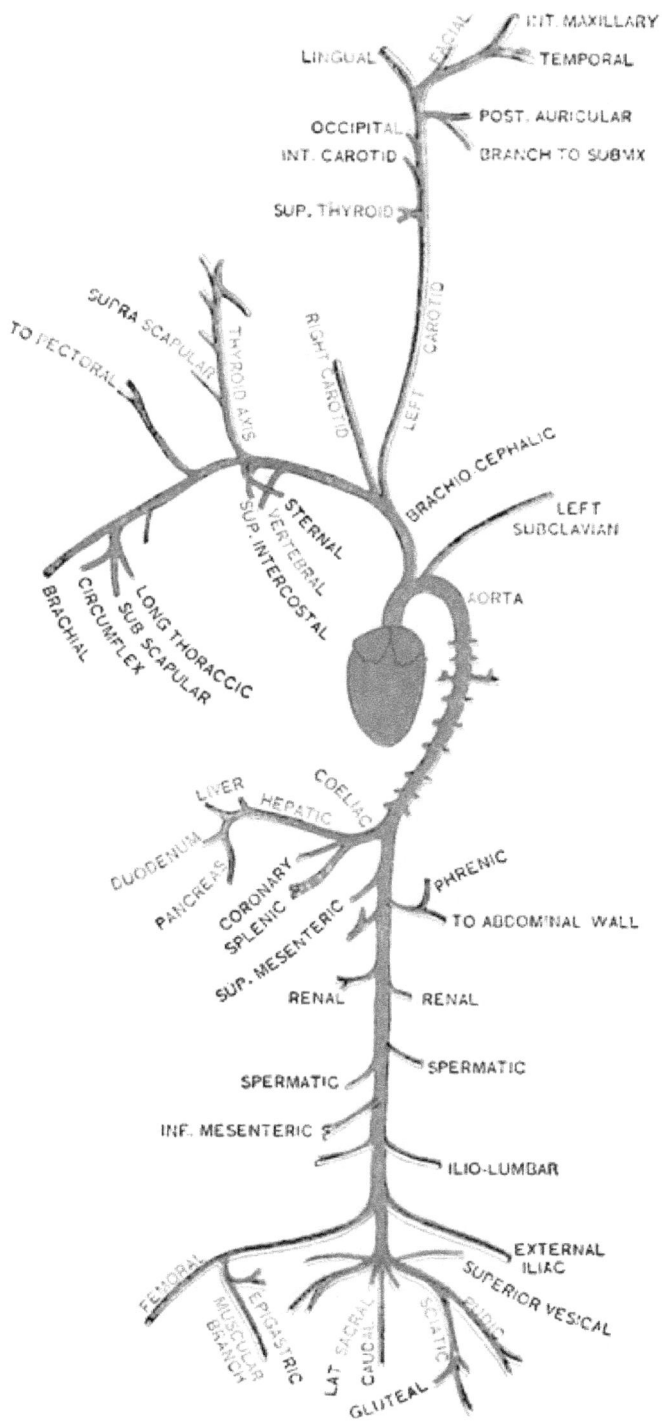

FIG. 4.—ARTERIAL SYSTEM OF THE DOG.

each side, going directly to the kidneys. The artery on the left side is somewhat posterior to that on the right. Each artery as it enters the hilus of the kidney splits into two or more branches.

7. **Muscular Branches.** Posterior to the renal arteries several muscular branches may arise which are distributed to the muscles of the abdominal wall.

8. **The Spermatic Arteries.** In the male they form two small branches of the aorta arising some distance posterior to the renals and going to the testes. They pass to the inguinal canal, and reach the testes in the spermatic cords. In the female they are known as the *ovarian arteries*, and pass more directly outward to reach these bodies, being distributed to them and to the anterior portion of the oviducts.

9. **The Inferior Mesenteric Artery** comes off from the aorta some distance posterior to the spermatics, and is distributed to the rectum and to the lower portion of the large intestine.

10. **The Iliac Arteries.** Below the inferior mesenteric the aorta divides into three branches, the two external iliacs and a median trunk ; this latter soon divides again into three branches, the two internal iliacs and a median sacral or caudal artery.

11. **The Internal Iliacs.** Open the pelvis as directed in the dissection of the reproductive organs. Each internal iliac gives off just beyond its origin a small branch, the *superior vesical*, which passes to the bladder ; each iliac then divides into two main branches, the *pudic* and the *sciatic*. The pudic lies more to the outer side ; followed out it breaks into two branches, one of which, the *internal pudic*, is distributed to the genital organs in the pelvis—in the female to the vagina, vestibule, and uterus ; the other seems to

correspond to the *external pudic*, being distributed to
the external genital organs. This arrangement is different from that in man.

The second chief division of the internal iliac, the
sciatic, after giving off two large branches, the *gluteals*,
which supply the muscles on the back of the pelvis,
passes along with the sciatic nerve through the sacro-
sciatic foramen to reach the exterior of the pelvis,
where it is distributed chiefly to muscles.

12. **The External Iliacs** pass beneath Poupart's ligament to reach the front of the thigh, where they are
known as the femoral arteries. Before leaving the
abdomen each gives off a large branch, which seems
to have no homologue in human anatomy. This
branch in turn gives off one or two branches, the
epigastric artery, which is distributed to the muscles
of the anterior abdominal wall, and then passes beneath Poupart's ligament to reach the inner portion
of the thigh, where it is distributed chiefly to the large
adductor muscles.

13. **The Femoral Artery** runs for some distance just
below the sartorius muscle, giving off several
branches to the muscles, and one long branch, the
saphenous artery, which passes to the leg, lying
below the skin. The femoral next bends sharply
inward to reach the back of the knee-joint, where it is
named the *popliteal artery;* this divides into two
branches, one rather large which passes into the leg
between the tibia and fibula, and finally reaches the
front of the leg. It corresponds to the *anterior tibial*
of human anatomy, and may be followed down upon
the dorsum of the foot. The second, smaller division
sends branches to the lower portions of the muscles

of the thigh and the gastrocnemius; it represents the *posterior tibial.*

B. VEINS BELONGING TO THE SYSTEM OF THE POST-CAVA.

1. **The Post-cava** (*inferior vena-cava*). Follow its course to the diaphragm. It receives no branches in the thoracic cavity.

2. **The Hepatic Veins.** Where the cava pierces the diaphragm it receives two hepatic veins, one usually larger than the other.

3. **The Phrenic Veins** empty into the cava at about the same level as the hepatic veins. They bring back blood from the diaphragm.

4. **The Renal Veins.** Follow the post-cava along the dorsal wall of the abdomen. At first it is partly imbedded in the liver; just below the liver it receives the two large renal veins coming directly from the kidneys. The left is slightly posterior to the right.

5. **The Spermatic** (*ovarian*) **Veins**, corresponding to the spermatic arteries. The one on the left side empties into the left renal vein, the one on the right side directly into the cava.

6. **The Iliac Veins.** Below the renal the cava receives several veins from the muscles of the abdominal wall, and finally divides into two large branches, the *common iliac veins.* Each of these in turn divides into an *external* and an *internal iliac vein* which bring back blood from the regions supplied by the arteries of the same name.

C. THE HEPATIC PORTAL SYSTEM OF VEINS.

The **Portal Vein** is the large vein lying in the mesentery which collects venous blood from the stomach, pancreas, spleen and intestines, and passes into the under side, of the liver. Within this organ it again breaks up into capillaries, the blood from which is finally collected into the hepatic veins which empty into the post-cava. The portal can easily be found on the under side of the liver; it is formed from two large branches, one from the intestines and one from the spleen, pancreas and stomach. It breaks up into branches which enter the different lobes of the liver.

D. VEINS BELONGING TO THE SYSTEM OF THE PRÆ-CAVA.

1. The **Præ-cava** (*superior vena-cava*). A description of this vein has been given in the chapter on the dissection of the thoracic viscera.

2. The **Vena Azygos.** Make out again the course of this vein, and the point where it opens into the præ-cava.

3. The **Vertebral Veins.** The vein on the right side opens into the cava anterior to the azygos. Trace it back to its emergence from the vertebral canal of the spinal column. The vein on the left side opens into the left brachio-cephalic or innominate vein. They bring back blood from the brain, etc.

4. The **Sternal Veins.** The vein on the right side opens into the præ-cava anterior to the vertebral. On the left side it opens into the brachio-cephalic beyond the vertebral. They bring back blood from the sternum and the anterior wall of the thorax.

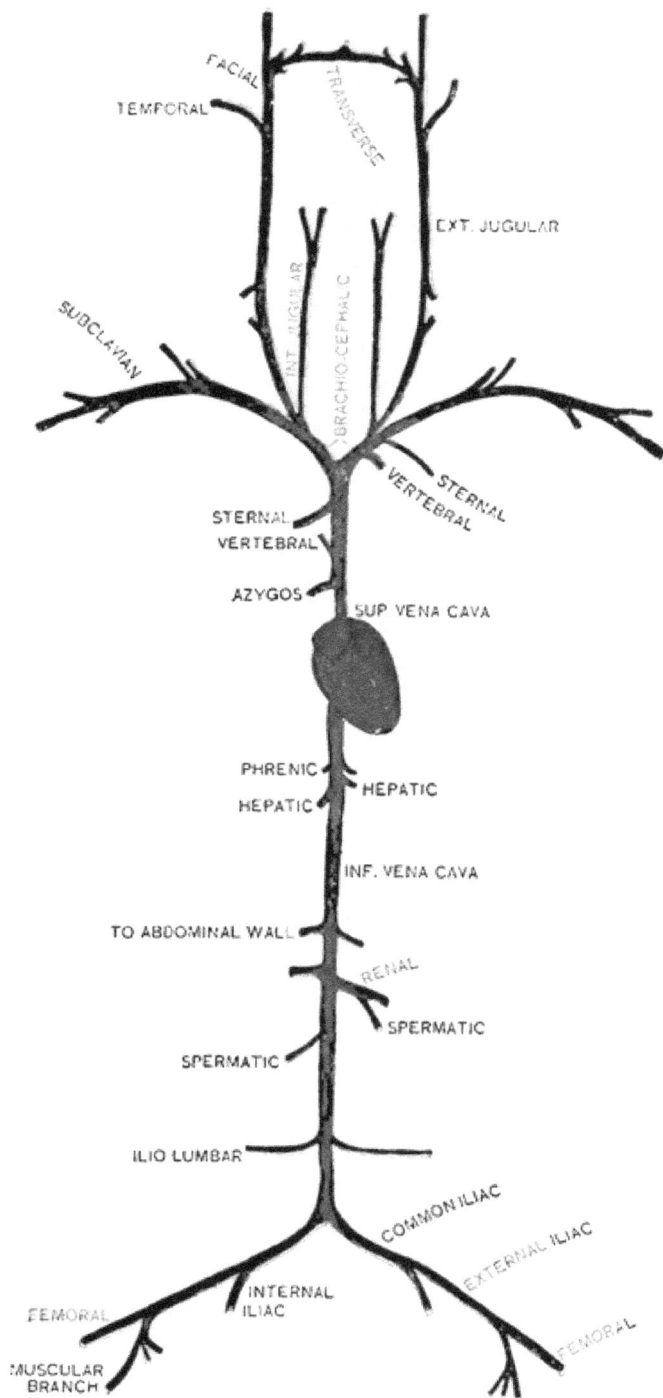

FIG. 5.—VENOUS SYSTEM OF THE DOG.

5. **The Brachio-cephalic** (*innominate*) **Veins.** The two large veins which unite to form the præ-cava. Each after a short course divides into the sub-clavian and external jugular.

6. **The Sub-clavian Vein** brings back blood from the arm, shoulder, etc. Beyond the point where it joins the external jugular it receives the *sub-scapular* vein. Followed into the arm it will be found to receive a number of muscular branches.

7. **The External Jugular** passes toward the head, lying just below the skin in its course through the neck. Near the level of the larynx the jugular divides into two branches, the *facial* and the *temporal*, bringing back blood from the head. The sub-maxillary gland lies between these two veins and sends a small vein to each of them. The facial veins of the two sides are united by a wide cross-branch—the *transverse* vein.

8. **The Internal Jugular.** Near the junction of the external jugular and sub-clavian the former receives the internal jugular, which has a deeper course along the side of the trachea. It brings back blood from the brain.

E. THE ARTERIES OF THE ANTERIOR POR-
TION OF THE BODY.

1. **The Arch of the Aorta.** Clean the fat, etc., from the arch. The following branches are given off from it :

2. **The Brachio-cephalic** (*innominate*) **Artery,** given off nearest to the heart.

3. **The Left Sub-clavian Artery,** given off separately, and distributed to the left arm, shoulder, etc.

4. **The Common Carotid Arteries.** Dissect out the brachio-cephalic trunk. The two common carotids

are given off separately though close together, and pass forward in the neck, one on each side of the trachea.

Make a median incision along the ventral surface of the neck from the larynx to the sternum. Clear away the muscles lying on the trachea and the common carotids will be exposed. Each gives off the following branches:

5. **The Superior Thyroid Artery,** given off at the level of the thyroid body, to which it is chiefly distributed.

6. **The Internal Carotid.** At the level of the larynx the common carotid divides into the internal and external carotid. The former is much smaller and passes to the base of the skull, which it enters through the carotid foramen, being one of the arteries which supplies the brain with blood.

7. **The External Carotid** seems to be the direct continuation of the common carotid. It gives off the following branches :

8. **The Occipital Artery** is a small branch arising close to the internal carotid and running parallel to it. It is distributed to the exterior of the skull in the occipital region.

9. **The Lingual Artery,** the third branch of the external carotid, is a large artery distributed chiefly to the tongue.

10. **The Facial Artery** is a small branch given off a short distance beyond the lingual. It usually gives a branch to the submaxillary gland.

11. **The Posterior Auricular,** the next branch, is given off from the outer side of the carotid, supplying the tissues on the posterior side of the ear. A short distance from its origin it may give a branch to the submaxillary gland.

12. **The Internal Maxillary Artery.** Just beyond the origin of the facial the external carotid divides into two branches, the larger being the internal maxillary, distributed to the inner side of the mandible, maxilla, etc.; the smaller branch is

13. **The Temporal Artery,** distributed to the muscles and integument of the side of the head.

14. **The Right Sub-clavian Artery.** Beyond the origin of the two common carotids the brachio-cephalic artery is known as the right sub-clavian artery. The chief branches are as follows:

15. **The Vertebral Artery,** a branch which passes dorsally to reach the vertebral canal of the spinal column, through which it reaches the interior of the skull to supply the brain.

16. **The Superior Intercostal Artery** comes off quite close to the vertebral, sometimes forming a branch of it. It is distributed to the three anterior ribs.

17. **The Sternal** (*internal mammary*) **Artery,** given off a little beyond the last. In company with the artery of the other side it passes along the under surface of the sternum, supplying it and the adjacent portions of the ribs.

18. **The Thyroid Axis** arises usually somewhat nearer the heart than the last, but from the anterior border of the sub-clavian. It seems to be homologous with the thyroid axis of human anatomy, but has a different distribution. It divides into branches which supply the muscles of the root of the neck and of the supra-scapular region.

19. **The Pectoral Branches.** Beyond the thyroid axis the sub-clavian artery, now known as the *axillary*, gives off one or two branches which are distributed chiefly to the pectoral muscle.

20. Near the point where the axillary artery enters the arm it gives off a large branch from its posterior border which divides into three arteries :

a. THE LONG THORACIC ARTERY, a small branch passing along the side of the thorax and distributed chiefly to the pectoral and latissimus dorsi muscles.

b. THE SUB-SCAPULAR ARTERY, a large branch distributed to the sub-scapular muscles.

c. The CIRCUMFLEX ARTERY, passing obliquely round the humerus and distributed chiefly to the triceps extensor muscle of the arm.

21. The Brachial Artery. After reaching the arm the axillary artery is known as the brachial. It gives off muscular branches in the arm, and at the elbow divides into two branches for the fore-arm.

CHAPTER V.

MUSCLES OF THE THORAX—DISSECTION OF THE NECK—THE SYMPATHETIC SYSTEM—THE BRACHIAL PLEXUS AND THE LARYNX.

MUSCLES OF THE THORAX.

Make a median incision through the skin of the thorax along the line of the sternum, and transverse incisions at the shoulders. Dissect off the flaps of skin from the thorax, shoulder, and upper part of the abdomen. In removing the skin notice the thin skin-muscle extending over the posterior and outer portion of the thorax and the abdomen. Remove the fat and fascia from the thorax, and the group of pectoralis muscles will be exposed.

1. **Pectoralis Major Muscle.** This name is applied to the large muscle arising from the sternum and ribs, and inserted into the humerus. In reality the muscle can be divided into five or more separate divisions or muscles, whose origin and insertion extend along the lines named. The two or three most anterior of these divisions arise from the anterior end of the sternum as far back as the junction of the 3d rib. They form a group of fibres which pass nearly transversely outward to be inserted into the middle and lower third of the shaft of the humerus. Cut across the fibres of this

band and reflect the cut ends; the remaining divisions of the pectoralis will be fully exposed. The fibres arise along the whole length of the sternum, pass obliquely forward and outward to be inserted into the head and upper part of the shaft of the humerus, and partly also into the fascia covering the biceps muscle of the arm.

Cut across the pectoralis muscle and reflect the cut ends.

2. The Sternalis Muscle is a small fan-shaped muscle lying lateral to the anterior end of the sternum. The muscular fibres arise at the level of the cartilaginous portion of the 2d and 3d ribs from a strong fascia; they pass obliquely forward and outward to be inserted into the 1st rib.

3. The Scaleni Muscles arise from the transverse processes of the last four cervical vertebræ, and are inserted into the ribs. In the dog four scaleni may be distinguished lying close to one another:

a. THE SCALENUS PRIMUS lies nearest to the ventral mid-line; it arises from the transverse processes of the 5th and 6th cervical vertebræ, and is inserted into the 1st rib where the bony and cartilaginous portions meet.

b. THE SCALENUS SECUNDUS is much longer; it arises from the transverse processes of the 4th and 5th cervical vertebræ by two tendons, and is inserted into the bony ribs from the 3d to the 7th.

c. THE SCALENUS TERTIUS lies dorsal to the anterior end of the secundus; it arises in common with it, but is inserted into the bony portion of the 1st rib to the outer side of the insertion of the primus.

d. THE SCALENUS QUARTUS is a very small muscle inserted into the 1st rib between the primus and tertius; it arises from the transverse process of the 7th cervical vertebra.

4. The Intercostal Muscles. Remove the above-named muscles and fat, etc., from the thorax; the intercostal muscles lying between the ribs will be exposed.

a. THE EXTERNAL INTERCOSTALS form the external layer passing from the posterior margin of one bony rib to the anterior margin of the succeeding one; the fibres have an inclination inward and to the posterior. This layer ceases at the cartilaginous ribs. The layer of muscle between these portions of the ribs forms the *intercartilaginous muscles*, and their fibres have an inclination in the opposite direction.

b. THE INTERNAL INTERCOSTALS. Dissect off the external intercostals between two or three of the ribs, and the internal intercostals will be exposed; these also pass from one bony rib to the other, but have an inclination outward and to the posterior.

DISSECTION OF THE NECK.

Make an incision along the mid-line of the neck through the skin, and the necessary transverse incisions at the shoulder. Lay back the flaps of skin on both sides.

1. **The Platysma Myoides** is a skin-muscle found in the neck which may have been reflected with the skin. The chief bundle of fibres in it arises from the dorsal wall of the anterior portion of the thorax, and comes obliquely around to the ventral surface of the neck, and continues forward to the head. Scattered muscular fibres pass transversely from this during its course toward the ventral mid-line of the neck. The muscle is attached only to the skin.

2. **The Hyoid Bone** lies just anterior to the larynx. Determine its shape by feeling through the muscles covering it. The body is a short transverse bar of bone, and from it two horns — posterior cornua — may be felt passing posteriorly to the thyroid cartilage of the larynx. Two longer anterior horns pass to the base of the skull to be attached to the temporal bone.

3. **The Sterno-mastoid Muscles** form a pair of broad muscular bands arising from the anterior end of the sternum, and passing obliquely forward, diverging from each other, to be inserted into the mastoid portion of the temporal bone.

Cut these muscles at the sternal insertion, and reflect them forward.

4. **The Sterno-hyoid Muscles,** one on each side, lie along the ventral mid-line of the neck. Separate the two along the mid-line, and the trachea will be exposed. Each is a flat band arising from the anterior end of the sternum and the 1st rib, and inserted into the hyoid bone.

Cut the sterno-hyoids at the anterior end and reflect backwards.

5. **Sterno-thyroid Muscles,** one on each side of the neck. Each is a slender band of muscle arising from the anterior end of the sternum with the *sterno-hyoids*, and passing obliquely forward to be inserted into the side of the thyroid cartilage of the larynx.

Cut the sterno-thyroids at the anterior end and reflect backwards ; the trachea will be fully exposed.

6. **The Thyroid Glands** are two oval bodies lying one on each side of the trachea just posterior to the larynx. Usually these are entirely separated from each other (differing in this respect from the same struct-

ures in man), but occasionally the posterior ends are connected by a slender band or isthmus passing across the trachea.

7. **The Mylo-hyoid Muscle** lies anterior to the hyoid bone, between the rami of the mandible. It is a thin muscular sheet which arises from the hyoid bone on each side, and is inserted along the inner side of the mandible; it meets its fellow in the mid-line and forms the floor of the mouth.

8. **The Digastric Muscle** is the thick muscle covering the angle and part of the body of the mandible. It arises from the occipital bone of the skull, and is inserted into the mandible, serving to depress the jaw. In the dog it is not truly a digastric muscle, though a tendinous line may be observed running across its belly somewhat posterior to the middle.

9. **The Vago-sympathetic Nerve.** The combined trunk of the vagus and sympathetic nerves lies along the trachea on each side, in the same sheath with the carotid artery and internal jugular vein. Expose it on the left side at the middle of the neck, and dissect it anteriorly. To expose its origin from the skull, cut the digastric muscle at its mandibular insertion and reflect it backward. When the parts are a little more dissected it will be well to remove this muscle entirely, taking care not to cut the hypoglossal nerve.

10. **The Superior Laryngeal Nerve** is a branch of the vagus; it arises far forward, somewhat beyond the anterior end of the larynx. At its origin from the vagus there is an enlargement of that nerve known as the ganglion of the trunk of the vagus. Trace the superior laryngeal to the larynx, which it enters and supplies with sensory fibres, giving also motor fibres to

one of the intrinsic muscles of the larynx, the crico-thyroid. The superior laryngeal anastomoses with the inferior laryngeal by a large branch passing beneath the wing of the thyroid cartilage.

11. Somewhat posterior to the origin of the superior laryngeal the sympathetic trunk separates from the vagus. Follow it forward a short distance until it ends in the *superior cervical ganglion*.

Just anterior to its ganglionic enlargement the vagus enters the skull. Emerging at about the same point the following cranial nerves can be found :

12. **The Hypoglossal, or 12th Cranial Nerve,** is very large ; it runs forward beneath the digastric and mylohyoid muscles to enter the tongue, to which it supplies motor fibres. It leaves the skull through the anterior condylar foramen.

a. THE DESCENDENS HYPOGLOSSI, a branch of the hypoglossal, arises from the convex border of the loop made by the hypoglossal and passes posteriorly along the neck superficial to the vagus and carotid ; in its course it soon unites with a branch of the first cervical spinal nerve, and from the common trunk branches are given to the sterno-thyroid and sterno-hyoid muscles. The nerve is very long, reaching to the posterior third of the neck.

13. **The Spinal Accessory. or 11th Cranial Nerve,** leaves the skull through the jugular foramen in company with the vagus and glosso-pharyngeal ; it runs posteriorly upon the sterno-mastoid muscle, within which it soon disappears. It supplies this and other muscles of the neck with motor fibres.

14. **The Glosso-pharyngeal, or 9th Cranial Nerve,** appears in the same place close to the vagus ; it turns inward to the mid-line and disappears in the muscles

enveloping the pharynx. It supplies the tongue and pharynx with sensory fibres, and gives some motor fibres also to the pharynx.

15. The Lingual Nerve. If not previously done, cut through the mylo-hyoid muscle ; the lingual will be exposed coming out from under the mandible. It runs toward the mid-line and disappears in the tongue, which it supplies with gustatory fibres. This nerve is a branch of the inferior maxillary division of the 5th or trigeminal nerve.

Continue the dissection of the vago-sympathetic trunk posteriorly. In order to show the relations of this trunk at the root of the neck and in the thorax, open the latter freely, as in the dissection of the thoracic viscera, double-ligature the large veins at the root of the neck, divide them between the ligatures, and then dissect out the vago-sympathetic trunk.

16. Inferior Cervical Ganglion. At the root of the neck the vago-sympathetic ends in a large ganglion, the *inferior cervical ganglion*, from which several small branches are given off, passing toward the heart and entering the cardiac plexus. At the ganglion the two nerves separate as shown in Fig. 6.

17. The Thoracic Vagus continues posteriorly from the ganglion, giving off also some small branches to join the cardiac plexus. Near the base of the heart it gives off a large branch, the *recurrent or inferior laryngeal*, which on the left side curves round the aorta and passes anteriorly along the side of the trachea in the neck, where it can easily be found and followed to its termination in the larynx, to the muscles of which it gives motor fibres. Dissect out the communicating branch to the superior laryngeal which passes beneath the wing of the thyroid cartilage. On the right side

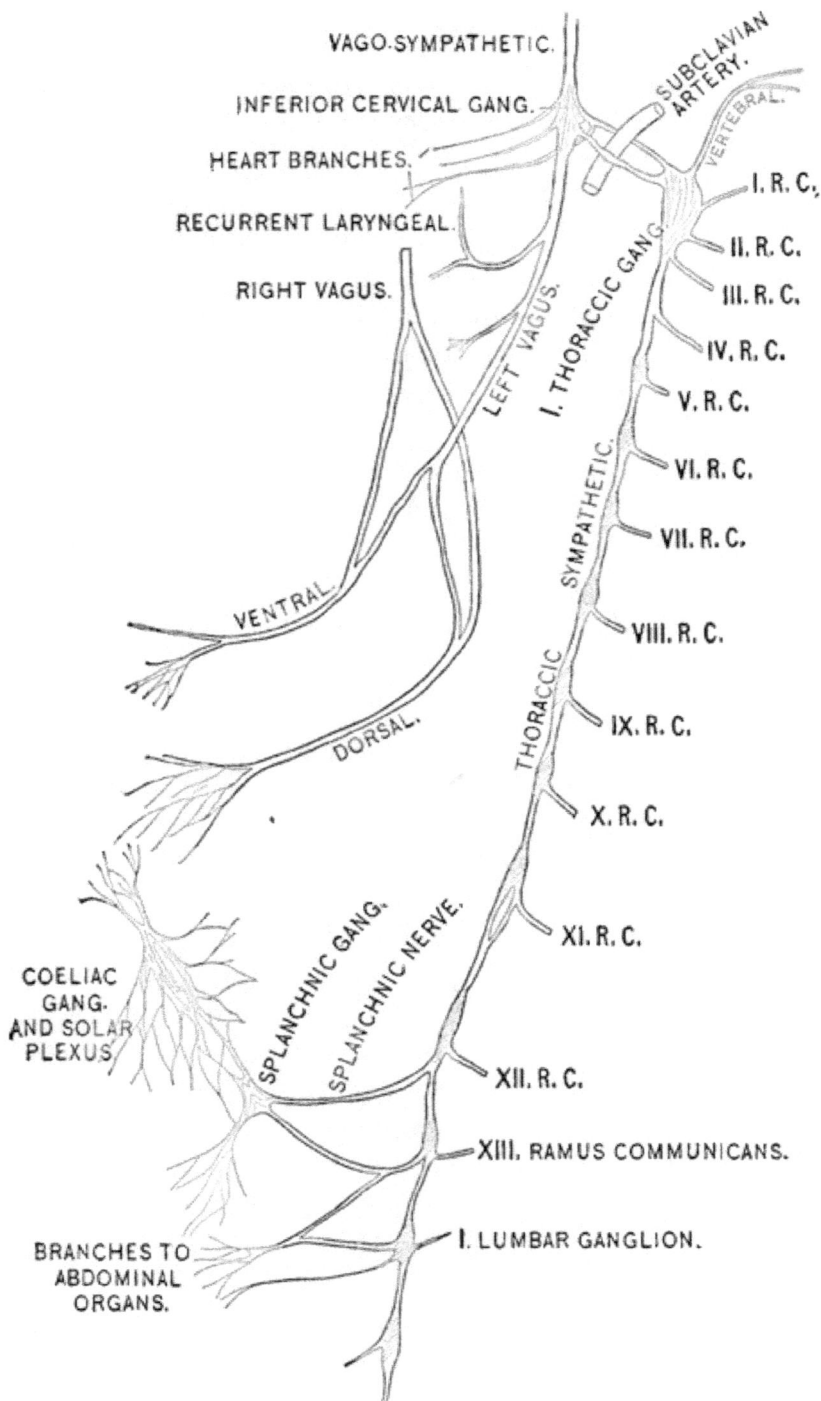

VAGO-SYMPATHETIC.

INFERIOR CERVICAL GANG.

HEART BRANCHES.

RECURRENT LARYNGEAL.

RIGHT VAGUS.

SUBCLAVIAN ARTERY.

VERTEBRAL.

LEFT VAGUS.

I. THORACIC GANG.

I. R. C.

II. R. C.

III. R. C.

IV. R. C.

V. R. C.

VI. R. C.

VII. R. C.

VIII. R. C.

IX. R. C.

X. R. C.

XI. R. C.

SYMPATHETIC.

THORACIC.

VENTRAL.

DORSAL.

SPLANCHNIC GANG.

SPLANCHNIC NERVE.

COELIAC GANG. AND SOLAR PLEXUS.

XII. R. C.

XIII. RAMUS COMMUNICANS.

I. LUMBAR GANGLION.

BRANCHES TO ABDOMINAL ORGANS.

Fig. 6.—Diagram of the Vagus and Sympathetic Nerves.

this nerve curves round the sub-clavian artery, and
then continues forward into the neck as described.
After giving off other branches to the lungs, the
vagus descends along the œsophagus, and finally
divides into two branches, one of which passes to the
dorsal side of the œsophagus, and is there joined by a
similar branch from the right vague ; the other division
passes to the ventral side of the œsophagus, where it
joins the similar ventral branch of the right vagus.
The two new trunks thus formed can be traced to the
stomach ; each ends in a plexus of nerve-fibres, which
are distributed to the stomach and make connections
also with the solar plexus of the cœliac ganglia.

18. The Thoracic Sympathetic Trunk. From the
inferior cervical ganglion two branches pass to the
large *1st thoracic ganglion,* one above and one
below the sub-clavian artery, forming a ring known as
the "*annulus of Vieussens.*" From this annulus one
or more small branches may be given off toward the
heart to join the cardiac plexus.

The 1st thoracic ganglion is very large, and besides
its connections with the inferior cervical gives off the
following branches: *a.* A large branch, the *vertebral,*
passing forward to join with the two lower cervical
spinal nerves. *b.* A branch to the 1st thoracic spinal
nerve. *c.* A branch to the 2d thoracic spinal. *d.* A
branch to the 3d thoracic spinal, and sometimes, *e,* a
branch to the 4th thoracic spinal.

From the 1st thoracic ganglion the sympathetic
trunk continues backward along the spinal column,
and at intervals shows ganglionic swellings, usually one
for each rib after the 3d or 4th ; but this is sometimes
irregular. From each ganglion a branch passes to the

corresponding spinal nerve.   These branches of communication are known as the *rami communicantes*.

In the posterior portion of the thorax, just after giving off a ramus communicans to the 12th or the 13th thoracic spinal nerve, the sympathetic sends off a large branch to the inner side, known as the *splanchnic nerve*.   This nerve passes through the diaphragm and (in the dog) ends in a ganglionic enlargement, the *splanchnic ganglion*.   From this ganglion small branches can be traced inward and forward, ending in a larger nerve-mass, the *cœliac ganglion*, which lies just posterior to the cœliac axis and on the ventral aspect of the aorta.   There is a similar arrangement on the other side, the two cœliac ganglia being connected with each other by cross-branches and sending very numerous fine branches to the surrounding abdominal organs, which form what is called the *solar plexus*. The solar plexus, as before mentioned, is connected with the terminal plexuses of the vagi.

After giving off the splanchnic the sympathetic may have one more ganglion in the thorax, from which a ramus communicans is given to the 13th thoracic spinal nerve, and a small branch, the *small splanchnic*, which joins the splanchnic ganglion.   It then passes through the diaphragm and continues as the abdominal sympathetic, which also has ganglionic enlargements as in the thorax.   From these ganglia branches arise which form plexuses, similar to the solar plexus, for the abdominal and pelvic organs.   The two sympathetic trunks finally unite at the posterior end of the sacrum in an unpaired ganglion lying in the mid-line.

19. The Brachial Plexus in the dog is formed from the 6th, 7th and 8th cervical spinal nerves and the 1st thoracic spinal nerve, and usually receives a small branch from the 2d thoracic spinal nerve. Shortly after emerging from the vertebral canal these nerves branch to form a complicated plexus, represented in Fig. 7, from which branches are given off to the arm, fore-arm, shoulder, etc. The plexus should be dissected upon the side the least injured by previous dissection; in this case probably the right side. **Cut**

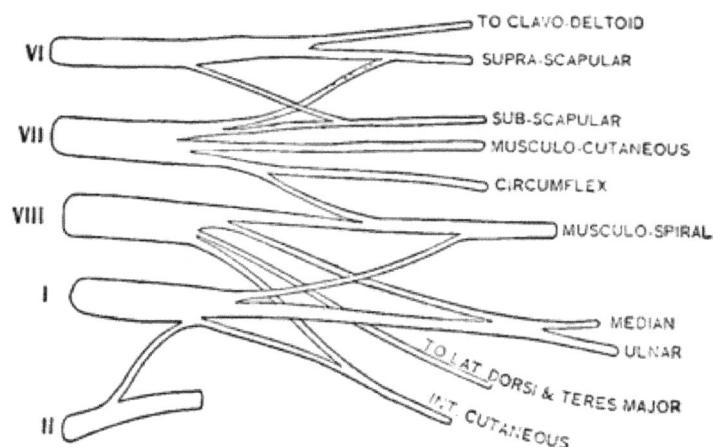

Fig. 7.—Diagram of the Brachial Plexus of the Dog.

carefully through the muscles on the side of the vertebral column where the neck and thorax meet until some of the nerves are exposed, and then from this trace out the other members of the plexus. In order to expose the plexus fully one must take great care not to cut small branches, and must dissect slowly. The following are the chief terminal branches of the plexus. From which of the spinal nerves they are derived can be seen from the figure, although the arrangement of the plexus varies somewhat in different individuals.

a. Branch distributed chiefly to the clavo-deltoid.

b. Supra-scapular Nerve to muscles on the dorsal side of the scapula.

c. Sub-scapular Nerve to muscles on the ventral side of the scapula.

d. Musculo-cutaneous Nerve supplies the biceps and may be traced finally to the elbow, where it breaks up into fibres distributed to the skin of the elbow and fore-arm.

e. Circumflex Nerve sends some branches to the teres major and the sub-scapular muscles, and then passes dorsally between the insertion of the teres major and the triceps, giving off branches to the triceps and the anterior deltoid muscles.

f. Musculo-spiral Nerve passes obliquely round the humerus to the dorsal side to reach the radial side of the fore-arm, where it divides into two branches, the radial and posterior inter-osseus nerves. It supplies the muscles and skin of the back of the arm, and in the fore-arm is distributed to the muscles and the digits of the radial side.

g. The Median Nerve.

h. The Ulnar Nerve. These two nerves arise together from the 8th cervical and 1st thoracic nerve; they pass to the fore-arm and hand, to which they are distributed.

i. A branch to the teres major and latissimus dorsi muscles.

k. The Interal Cutaneous Nerve. Besides giving some branches to the pectoral muscles this is distributed to the skin on the inner side of the arm.

20. The Intrinsic Muscles of the Larnyx.

To dissect these muscles it is better to remove the larynx and epiglottis entirely from the body. Cut

*through the trachea below the larynx and through the
pharynx above the hyoid bone ; in taking out the larynx
dissect it free from the œsophagus, which adheres to its
dorsal side. The intrinsic laryngeal muscles form six
pairs, and with the exception of the arytenoid muscles
correspond very well to those of human anatomy. The
illustrations in the text-book of human anatomy may
therefore be consulted if necessary.*

a. THE CRICO-THYROID MUSCLE is a short triangular
muscle arising from the ventral and lateral faces of the
cricoid, and is inserted into the posterior border of the
thyroid and its posterior cornu.

b. THE POSTERIOR CRICO-ARYTENOID MUSCLE arises
from the flattened dorsal surface of the cricoid, and
is inserted into the arytenoid cartilages, the fibres
passing obliquely forward and outward.

c. THE LATERAL CRICO-ARYTENOID is concealed by
the wing of the thyroid. Cut through the posterior
horn of the thyroid where it joins the cricoid and
lift up the wing of the thyroid. The muscle is seen as
a band of fibres arising from the lateral surface of the
cricoid, and passing obliquely toward the dorsal side
to be inserted into the arytenoid.

d. THE THYRO-ARYTENOID MUSCLE is anterior to
the last, the fibres having somewhat the same general
direction. It consists of two nearly separate muscular
bands which arise from the internal face of the ventral
portion of the thyroid and pass dorsally to be inserted
into the arytenoid.

e. THE ARYTENO-EPIGLOTTIDEAN lies anterior to the
last and nearly parallel with it. It arises from the
arytenoid cartilage and passes ventrally and forward
to end in the aryteno-epiglottidean fold. The muscles

of the two sides at their origin are connected by a cross-slip of muscular fibres.

f. THE ARYTENOID MUSCLE. The fleshy portion arises from the arytenoid cartilage just anterior to the insertion of the posterior crico-arytenoid, and is inserted into the inner angle of the arytenoid of the opposite side.

CHAPTER VI.

DISSECTION OF THE BRAIN.

The brain should be removed immediately after killing the dog, and placed in alcohol for a week or longer before dissecting. To prevent flattening wrap the brain in raw cotton before placing it in the alcohol.

To remove the brain, first skin the head, and cut off the muscles attached to the skull especially in the occipital region. Then with a small hand-saw carefully saw through the bone in a horizontal plane round the skull so as to isolate the cap of the skull. With a little care this can be done without tearing the brain at all. Remove the cap and with bone forceps chip off as much of the sides of the skull as is necessary to fully uncover the brain. Take out the brain by lifting it up carefully from either end, and cutting the nerves that come off from the ventral surface. Cut the nerves so as to leave as much of a stump as possible adhering to the brain.

In addition to the brain hardened in alcohol it will be convenient to harden two other brains in Muller's or

Erlicki's* liquid for a month or more, then wash them well in water and keep in 80° alcohol. One should be divided longitudinally by a cut through the great longitudinal fissure and the corpus callosum, and the other should be divided into a series of cross-sections, each about ½ in. thick, from the anterior to the posterior end of the brain. After having dissected an alcohol brain according to the following directions the study of these cross and longitudinal sections will prove very instructive in giving the proper relations of the different parts to one another.

A.　THE BRAIN MEMBRANES.

1. The Dura Mater will be exposed in removing the brain. It is the tough membrane lining the inside of the skull. It projects in between the lobes of the cerebrum as a vertical fold, the *falx cerebri*, and as a transverse fold, the *tentorium*, between the cerebrum and cerebellum.

2. The Pia Mater is a much thinner membrane, closely investing the brain; it is very vascular, since the blood-vessels supplying the brain are carried in it.

---

* The composition of these liquids is as follows :

MÜLLER'S LIQUID.

Water	100 parts.
Potassium bichromate	2 parts.
Sodium sulphate	1 part.

ERLICKI'S LIQUID.

Water	100 parts.
Potassium bichromate	2½ parts.
Copper sulphate	½ part.

The brains should be immersed in a relatively large quantity of these liquids, and during the first week of the hardening the liquid should be changed either every day or every second day. The Erlicki's liquid acts more quickly and is probably the better one of the two to use.

B. EXTERNAL CHARACTERS OF THE BRAIN.

1. The Dorsal Surface of the Brain.

a. THE CEREBRAL HEMISPHERES occupy the greater portion of the dorsal surface. They show a number of well-marked fissures and convolutions (sulci and gyri). The two hemispheres are connected by a broad white commissure, the *corpus callosum,* which may be seen by gently separating the two hemispheres and tearing or cutting away the pia mater which stretches across from one to the other. The corpus lies well toward the ventral surface of the hemispheres.

b. THE OLFACTORY LOBES are a pair of large flattened triangular lobes projecting from the ventral surface of the brain, but visible in a dorsal view.

c. THE CORPORA QUADRIGEMINA may be exposed by pressing apart the cerebellum and the cerebrum, and tearing away the intervening pia mater. They consist of two pairs of rounded elevations, of which the posterior pair are the larger.

d. THE CEREBELLUM. The whole surface is marked with narrow folds which run both in a transverse and a longitudinal direction. They are seen better if the pia mater is stripped off. The cerebellum is divided into a large median lobe, the *vermis,* in which the folds run transversely, and two lateral lobes or *hemispheres* in which the folds have a general longitudinal direction. On the outer and under sides of the hemispheres the loose *floccular lobes* will be seen if the brain has been carefully removed.

With a pair of forceps tear away carefully the pia mater beneath and posterior to the cerebellum to bring into view the medulla oblongata.

e. THE MEDULLA OBLONGATA lies beneath and

posterior to the cerebellum, and posteriorly passes into the spinal cord. Anteriorly the medulla widens out to form the *fourth ventricle*, which lies immediately under the cerebellum. This lozenge-shaped or oval cavity is covered over anteriorly by a thin sheet of nervous matter, the *valve of Vieussens* or the *anterior medullary velum*, easily seen, by pressing backward the cerebellum, as a thin membrane running from the posterior border of the corpora quadrigemina over the anterior part of the fourth ventricle. Posteriorly the fourth ventricle is roofed in by a similar membrane lying immediately under the cerebellum and probably removed in exposing the ventricle, the *posterior medullary velum*.

f. FLOOR OF THE FOURTH VENTRICLE. About the middle are seen two transverse bands of fibres—*medullary or auditory striæ*—the origin of the auditory nerve. The posterior end of the ventricle where the lateral walls converge is known as the *calamus scriptorius*.

g. FASCICULI OF THE MEDULLA OBLONGATA. Posterior to the calamus scriptorius the dorsal surface of the medulla shows a median fissure continuous with the posterior median fissure of the cord. On each side of this lies a rounded eminence, the *fasciculus gracilis* (posterior pyramid). Just exterior to this on each side is the small *fasciculus cuneatus*. If these two fasciculi are followed forward they run into a rounded eminence on each side, forming the lateral boundary of the fourth ventricle, the *restiform bodies*, and these followed anteriorly are seen to pass up into the cerebellum, forming the *posterior peduncles of the cerebellum*, making a connection between the cerebellum and cord.

2. The Ventral Surface of the Brain.

a. THE CEREBRAL HEMISPHERES meet in front, but diverge posteriorly. The vertical fissure separating the hemispheres (on the dorsal side) is continued around for some distance on the ventral surface. Note the large *olfactory lobes* lying along the ventral surface.

b. THE OPTIC CHIASMA. Lying at the end of the fissure is a transverse band of nerve-fibres, the chiasma. The *optic nerves* arise from it anteriorly, and posteriorly it passes backward and outward, forming the *optic tracts*, which finally end in the corpora quadrigemina. By carefully lifting up the side of the cerebral hemisphere each tract may be followed as it passes over the optic thalamus, in which some of the fibres end, until it reaches the corpora quadrigemina.

c. THE LAMINA CINEREA is exposed by turning back the optic chiasma. As will be seen later, it forms the anterior wall of the third ventricle. If gently torn, the third ventricle will be exposed.

d. THE INFUNDIBULUM lies immediately behind the chiasma. It is a median prolongation of the ventral surface of the brain : at its apex is the *pituitary body*. The infundibulum is hollow within, the cavity being a prolongation of the third ventricle.

e. THE CORPORA ALBICANTIA are two small white eminences posterior to the infundibulum.

f. THE CRURA CEREBRI are the two eminences lying outside of and posterior to the corpora albicantia. They pass forward and upward into the cerebral hemispheres, diverging from each other ; they form the connection between the cerebral hemispheres and the medulla. (To expose them clearly the pia mater must be cleaned off, taking care not to injure the cranial nerves.)

g. THE PONS VAROLII is the large band of transverse fibres lying back of the crura cerebri. It consists of transverse commissural fibres connecting the two sides of the cerebellum. Followed up toward the dorsal side it will be seen to pass into the cerebellum on each side, forming the *middle peduncles of the cerebellum*.

h. CORPUS TRAPEZOIDEUM, a band of similar transverse fibres lying posterior to the pons, and interrupted in the mid-line by the *anterior pyramids*.

i. THE ANTERIOR PYRAMIDS, the two bands of longitudinal fibres lying on the ventral surface of the medulla and ending (apparently) anteriorly in the pons. The anterior median fissure also ends at the pons.

3. The Roots of the Twelve Cranial Nerves.

a. THE OLFACTORY or I. cranial nerves arise from the under side of the olfactory lobes; most probably they were torn off in removing the brain.

b. THE OPTIC or II. cranial nerves arise from the anterior border of the optic chiasma.

c. THE OCULO-MOTOR or III. cranial nerves arise in the space between the two crura cerebri.

d. THE PATHETICUS or IV. cranial nerve is very small, and on the ventral surface appears in the space between the cerebral hemisphere and the crus cerebi on each side. The real origin is from the valve of Vieussens on the dorsal side of the brain. It may be followed back easily to this point.

e. THE TRIGEMINAL or V. cranial nerve is very large, and arises from the sides of the pons by two roots. The smaller, inner one is the motor root; the larger, outer one the sensory root.

f. THE ABDUCENS or VI. cranial nerve is small, and

arises from the ventral surface of the medulla back of the pons.

g. THE FACIAL or VII. cranial nerve arises from the outer side of the anterior border of the corpus trapezoideum behind the origin of the trigeminal.

h. THE AUDITORY or VIII. cranial nerve arises just outside of and behind the facial nerve. It is larger than the facial.

i. THE GLOSSOPHARYNGEAL AND THE VAGUS, the IX. and the X. cranial nerves, arise together by a number of slender roots from the side of the medulla behind and to the outer side of the origin of the auditory nerve.

j. THE SPINAL ACCESSORY or XI. cranial nerve arises by a number of roots from the side of the cord and medulla, extending forward as far as the origin of the vagus nerve.

k. THE HYPOGLOSSAL or XII. cranial nerve arises from the ventral surface of the medulla close to the mid-line and just outside of the anterior pyramids.

C. *THE INTERNAL STRUCTURE OF THE BRAIN.*

1. **The Cerebral Hemispheres** (*Fore-brain or prosencephalon*).

With a razor kept wet with alcohol take off horizontal slices of the cerebral hemispheres, cutting carefully until the corpus callosum is reached.

a. Note the structure of the cerebral hemispheres: the outer *cortical* layer of gray matter folded into the interior at the sulci, and the inner or medullary portion of white matter—nerve-fibres.

b. Notice the direction of the fibres of the corpus callosum, running transversely from one hemisphere to the other.

Remove carefully with forceps and knife the corpus callosum until the lateral ventricles are exposed, taking care not to injure the fornix, which lies immediately beneath.

c. THE LATERAL VENTRICLES, one on each side, fully exposed after complete removal of the corpus callosum. In each three chambers or horns may be distinguished; the *anterior cornu*, a narrow slit running forward and separated from the anterior cornu of the other side by a vertical partition—the *septum lucidum*; the *descending cornu*, situated posteriorly and curving downward and outward; the *posterior cornu*, situated at the most posterior end of the ventricle, a small diverticulum running backward, very inconspicuous in the dog.

d. THE SEPTUM LUCIDUM is the vertical partition lying between the anterior cornua of the two ventricles. It contains within its walls a small cavity, the so-called 5th ventricle, not formed by the closing in of the embryonic medullary tube like the other true ventricles of the brain.

e. THE CORPUS STRIATUM is the oval mass projecting into each anterior cornu from the side of the cerebral hemisphere. Only a part of the corpus striatum is seen in the dissection; the remainder is concealed in the walls of the hemisphere. It is originally an outgrowth from the floor of the vesicle of the cerebral hemispheres, and contains two nuclei of gray matter in its interior—the *nucleus caudatus*, contained within the part which projects into the ventricle, and the *nucleus lenticularis*, contained within the part buried in the wall of the hemisphere.

Lay open the descending cornu on one side by carefully cutting away the sides of the cerebral hemisphere.

Note its extensive course, sweeping around downward and forward to the bottom of the temporal lobe of the hemisphere.

f. The Hippocampus Major is the prominent convex ridge lying along the floor of the descending cornu.

g. The Fornix. The *posterior pillar of the fornix* is the narrow band of white fibres lying along the anterior border of the hippocampus major. The posterior pillars on each side followed forward meet just at the posterior edge of the septum lucidum, and unite for a short distance to form the *body* of the fornix; then bending downward they diverge again, forming the *anterior pillars* of the fornix, which run toward the base of the brain.

Cut away the outer wall of the anterior cornu on the same side on which the wall of the posterior cornu was removed.

h. The Foramen of Monro, one on each side, is the slit-like opening underneath the body and anterior pillar of the fornix. It leads into the 3d ventricle, and is the passage of communication between the 3d and the lateral ventricles.

To expose the 3d ventricle lift up carefully the posterior pillars of the fornix where they converge and tear them away with the forceps Remove in the same way the portion of the corpus callosum still left between the posterior pillars of the fornix and forming the roof of the 3d ventricle.

Properly speaking, the corpus callosum does not form the roof of the 3d ventricle. The true roof of the ventricle is a portion of the pia mater known as the *velum interpositum* which lies immediately beneath the corpus callosum. The velum interpositum

gets into the interior through the great transverse
fissure of the brain between the cerebrum and cerebellum.   At the anterior end of the ventricle it continues on through the foramen of Monro on each
side into the lateral ventricles, forming the *choroid
plexuses.*   Each choroid plexus is a thin vascular fold
of membrane which passes backward into the descending horn of the lateral ventricle upon the hippocampus
major.   If the corpus callosum is removed with sufficient care these relations of the pia mater can easily
be demonstrated upon the dog's brain.

i. The 3d Ventricle is seen as a narrow slit beginning just back of the anterior pillars of the fornix,
and extending posteriorly as far as the corpora
quadrigemina.   While narrow from side to side, it is
quite deep.

2. The Optic Thalami (*thalamencephalon*) are the
two oval masses forming the sides of the 3d ventricle.

a. The Pineal Gland is connected by a stalk to
the upper and posterior end of the 3d ventricle.   It
was originally a diverticulum from this ventricle.

b. The Commissures of the 3d Ventricle.

The *Middle Commissure* is very large, but delicate
and easily broken.   It passes across the middle of the
ventricle between the optic thalami.

The *Posterior Commissure* is at the extreme posterior end of the 3d ventricle, lying beneath the stalk
of the pineal gland ;   It is a narrow band of white fibres.

The *Anterior Commissure* lies at the extreme anterior end of the 3d ventricle, just where the anterior
pillars begin to diverge from each other.   By cutting
the body of the fornix open vertically this commissure can be brought into full view.   It is a narrow
band of white fibres.

Cutting through the middle commissure, the 3d ventricle can be seen to pass downward and forward toward the base of the brain, ending finally in the infundibulum. This can be seen best in a median longitudinal section of the brain. Posteriorly the 3d ventricle passes into the *aqueduct of Sylvius* just beneath the posterior commissure. A bristle can be passed backward easily along the aqueduct into the 4th ventricle.

By separating the posterior portion of the cerebral hemisphere completely from the optic thalamus a good view of the latter can be obtained, and the way in which the optic tract comes around from the ventral surface of the brain to end partly in the thalamus and partly in the corpora quadrigemina is nicely shown.

3. The Mid-brain or Mesencephalon.

a. THE CORPORA QUADRIGEMINA. They form the dorsal surface of the mid-brain, and surround the aqueduct of Sylvius.

b. THE CRURA CEREBRI form the base of the midbrain. They can be seen passing forward from the anterior border of the pons to the optic thalamus.

THE ANTERIOR CRURA OF THE CEREBELLUM pass forward along the sides of the 4th ventricle from the cerebellum to the corpora quadrigemina. The middle and posterior crura have already been seen, but ought to be located again at this point to get a complete idea of all the connections of the cerebellum.

CHAPTER VII.

DISSECTION OF THE EYE.

ACCESSORY ORGANS OF THE EYE.

With a moistened sponge clean the exposed portion of the eyeball and the eyelids from dirt.

1. **The Eyelids.** The upper and lower eyelids diverge from each other, leaving an oval space through which the front of the eyeball is seen. The points at which the two lids meet are known as the inner and outer angles or canthi of the eye.

2. **The Meibomian Glands.** On the inner margin of the edge of each lid will be seen a number of short yellowish lines passing inward for a short distance, arranged at right angles to the free edge : these are the Meibomian glands.

3. **The Conjunctiva.** The under or inner surface of each lid is covered by a loose mucous membrane, the conjunctiva. Follow this backward into the orbit ; it is soon reflected upon the surface of the eyeball, covering over the whole of the exposed portion. The conjunctival mucous membrane consists then of two parts, one covering the inner surface of the eyelids and one the external surface of the eyeball. The line along which the mucous membrane is reflected from

the eyelids to the eyeball is known as the *fornix con-junctivæ*. The portion of the conjunctiva upon the eyeball can be followed forward easily as far as the cornea. Upon the cornea itself it is reduced to a simple layer of stratified epithelial cells firmly adherent to the proper substance of the cornea, and visible only in microscopic sections.

4. **The Membrana Nictitans.** The third eyelid or nictitating membrane is very conspicuous in the dog. It is formed by a fold of the conjunctiva strengthened by a lamina of cartilage, and projects from the inner angle of the eye. In the dead animal it may extend over one third or one half of the exposed portion of the eyeball. In the human eye this membrane is reduced to a comparatively inconspicuous fold, the *plica semilunaris*.

5. **The Harderian Gland.** This gland lies on the inner face of the nictitating membrane. It is easily exposed by everting the membrane. It is not present in man.

6. **The Puncta Lacrymalia.** On the free edge of each eyelid, about 2 mm. or more from the inner canthus of the eye, are the mouths of two small ducts. Each begins as a small opening on the edge of the lid which leads into a short canal. The two canals end in an expanded portion known as the *lachrymal sac*, from which the *nasal duct* is continued downward to open into the lower portion of the nasal cavity. By means of this apparatus the tears which moisten the front of the eyeball are drained off into the nose, and thence into the pharynx.

7. **The Lachrymal Gland.** To expose the tear-gland cut through the skin and conjunctiva outward from the outer canthus for a short distance, and then

through the conjunctiva along the line of the fornix conjunctivæ of the upper lid. The lachrymal gland will be exposed lying on the upper and outer surface of the eyeball, between it and the tendinous margin of the orbit. Its ducts open upon the eyeball along the fornix conjunctivæ.

MUSCLES OF THE EYEBALL.

Remove the skin from the head. To expose the orbital cavity remove the zygomatic arch by sawing through it at its two ends and dissecting it off from the underlying parts. Next dissect away the muscular mass lying beneath the zygoma and on the side of the skull; in doing this it will be necessary to cut through and remove the coronoid process of the mandible, using the bone forceps. The eyeball with its cone-shaped mass of muscles running backward from it will now be exposed; all other tissues, muscle, fat, etc., must be dissected away as carefully as possible.

Six eye-muscles are usually described, namely, the internal and external rectus, the superior and inferior rectus, and the superior and inferior oblique. The dog has in addition a representative of the large retractor bulbi lying beneath the six muscles mentioned. No special directions can be given for dissecting out these various muscles. The student should read over first the descriptions of all of them, and then dissect as neatly as possible. None of the muscles will be difficult to expose except the superior oblique, which is very liable to be injured or overlooked; the upper and inner angle of the orbit, therefore, where its tendon is reflected to the eyeball must be dissected with particular care.

1. **The External Rectus Muscle** lies on the outer surface of the eyeball; it arises from the bony portion of the orbit round the optic foramen, and is inserted by a flat tendon into the outer surface of the eyeball beneath the conjunctiva.

2. **The Inferior Rectus Muscle** lies along the lower surface of the eyeball, and has the same general insertion and origin as the internal rectus, arising also from the bone round the optic foramen where the optic nerve enters the orbit. Its fibres do not lie exactly along the vertical meridian of the eyeball, so that its contraction will not rotate the eyeball directly downward.

3. **The Superior Rectus Muscle** lies along the upper surface of the eyeball; it arises also from the bone round the optic foramen, and is inserted into the eyeball on its upper surface. Owing to the direction of its fibres its pull will not rotate the eyeball directly upwards. Along the inner edge of this muscle a muscular slip may be seen, passing to the inner and upper angle of the orbit; this slip forms part of the levator palpebrae superioris, not one of the muscles of the eyeball.

4. **The Internal Rectus Muscle** lies along the inner side of the eyeball. It arises from the bone round the optic foramen, and passes forward to be inserted into the inner aspect of the eyeball.

5. **The Inferior Oblique Muscle** will be found along the lower and outer side of the front of the eyeball. Its fibres arise from the front portion of the floor of the orbit, from the orbital portion of the maxillary bone, and passing outward obliquely round the eyeball are inserted over the tendon of the external rectus muscle.

6. **The Superior Oblique Muscle.** The muscular

portion of this muscle lies to the inside of the internal rectus, between it and the inner wall of the orbit; its fibres arise round the optic foramen with the recti muscles, pass outward along the inner wall of the orbit to its upper and outer angle, where they end in a slender tendon which lies in a groove in a piece of cartilage (the trochlea) found at this point. After passing through the groove the tendon bends backward to the eyeball, and is inserted just beneath the tendon of the superior rectus muscle. The trochlea serves as a pulley to change the direction of the pull of the muscle.

7. **The Retractor Bulbi.** Lifting up the four recti muscles, or removing them altogether, there will be found beneath four slips of much paler muscle, having the same general direction as the recti muscles. Taken together they form the retractor bulbi, and in some mammals are united to form a single hollow muscle inserted round the circumference of the eyeball.

DISSECTION OF THE EYEBALL.

The dissection of the eyeball can be made upon the dog, or perhaps more conveniently upon one of the ordinary slaughter-house animals, the eyes of which can be obtained very easily from a butcher. Of the animals killed by butchers the pig has the best eye for dissection. While it is smaller than that of the ox or sheep, it is quite large enough to make it easy to dissect, and has the advantage of resembling the human eye more closely in size and general shape, and besides, like the human eye, has no tapetum, so that the anatomy of the retina is more clearly seen. The following directions are written especially for the pig's eye, though they can be used for the eyes of other mammals. Each student should be provided with two eyes, and care should be taken to have the eyes removed from the pig before it is scalded by the butcher for the purpose of removing the hair.

No student should attempt to dissect the eyeball before reading carefully in one of the human anatomies an account of its structure. The eye should be dissected in a wide pan with a layer of bees-wax upon the bottom, and as much of the dissection as possible should be done under water.

Dissect off the muscles fat, etc., adhering to the eyeball, leaving only the optic nerve. In cleaning the eyeball notice the conjunctival membrane on the anterior portion of the eyeball, and the ease with which it can be dissected off. Notice also that the optic nerve enters the eyeball to the inside and not at the middle point.

1. **The Sclerotic Coat** is the tough white connective-tissue coat covering over the greater portion of the eyeball. Anteriorly it passes suddenly into

2. **The Cornea,** the transparent membrane covering the front of the eyeball. Through it can be seen the *iris*, with its circular opening, the *pupil*. In the dead eye the pupil is usually very much enlarged from the dilatation of the iris.

Fasten the eyeball to the bottom of the dissecting-pan by passing a pin through the optic nerve. With a pair of forceps pinch up a piece of the sclerotic and cut through it with the scissors. The sclerotic is rather loosely attached to the underlying choroid coat, except at the entrance of the optic nerve and near the cornea, so that it can be cut through without injury to the choroid. Starting from the hole thus made, dissect off a wide strip of the sclerotic extending from the optic nerve to the cornea.

3. **The Choroid Coat** lying under the sclerotic is much thinner and very darkly pigmented. Beneath the line of junction of the sclerotic and cornea the choroid passes into the iris.

Pinch up a bit of the choroid with the forceps and snip it off with scissors. From this opening pull or dissect off the choroid from the whitish underlying retina.

4. **The Retina** will be exposed as a delicate opaque membrane lying upon the vitreous humor.

5. **The Vitreous Humor.** Pull off the retina with a pair of forceps. The vitreous humor will be seen as a transparent gelatinous mass filling up the cavity of the eyeball. It is enclosed in a delicate membrane, the *hyaloid membrane.* Through the window thus made the interior of the eyeball can be seen.

To get a better view of the interior cut through the eyeball in the equatorial plane with a pair of scissors, dividing it into an anterior and a posterior half.

POSTERIOR HALF.

6. **The Retina.** Notice the way in which the retina curls away from the choroid. One of the layers of the retina, the pigmentary epithelium, is left in connection with the choroid.

7. **The Optic Disc.** The point of entrance of the optic nerve is seen as a small white oval area, composed of the nerve-fibres of the optic nerve, and not having the structure of the retinal membrane. It is the blind spot of the eye. The blood-vessels of the retina enter through the optic nerve and can be seen radiating from the middle of the optic disc. The retina can be torn off easily with forceps as far as the optic disc, where it is firmly attached.

8. The Choroid Coat. After removing the retina a good view will be obtained of the choroid. This coat can also be torn off with but little difficulty from the sclerotic, except at the entrance of the optic nerve. Notice the difference in thickness between the two coats.

THE ANTERIOR HALF.

Looking into the anterior half, the crystalline lens will be seen through the vitreous humor, and through it the iris and pupil.

9. The Ciliary Processes of the Choroid. Surrounding the lens the anterior portion of the choroid coat is thrown into a number of radiating folds, the ciliary processes.

10. Ora Serrata of the Retina. The retinal coat ends round the periphery of the ciliary processes. The line of demarcation seems quite sharp, but if examined more closely with a lens it will be found to be wavy. This indented margin of the retina is the *ora serrata.* In reality there is a delicate membrane, continuous with the retina, extending forward from the ora serrata to the tips of the ciliary processes, known as the "pars ciliaris retinae," which is embryologically a part of the retina but does not have the true retinal structure.

11. The Crystalline Lens. Remove as much as possible of the vitreous humor without disturbing the lens; then with the point of the scissors raise the periphery of the lens from the ciliary processes: the delicate membrane passing from one to the other is the suspensory ligament of the lens. Remove the lens entirely and notice its shape. The posterior surface is much more convex than the anterior surface.

Divide this portion of the eye into a right and a, left half by a cut along the vertical meridian.

12. Junction of the Choroid and Iris. Along the cut edge of one of these halves notice the relations of the choroid, ciliary processes, and iris. The iris is directly continuous with the choroid, and along the line of junction of the two the part of the choroid coat known as the ciliary processes is partly free, projecting somewhat toward the interior of the eye.

13. The Canal of Schlemm. Find the point of junction of choroid and iris. Between this and the sclerotic where it joins the cornea is a rather conspicuous canal running circularly round the eyeball. Insert a bristle and follow its course.

14. The Ciliary Muscle. At the posterior margin of the canal of Schlemm the choroid coat is firmly attached to the sclerotic by an oblique band of whitish fibres, the radial fibres of the ciliary muscle. These fibres belong to the class of involuntary muscle-fibres. When they contract they pull forward the choroid coat and slacken the suspensory ligament, allowing the lens to become more convex.

For the following dissection a fresh eye should be used. Do not clean off the muscles, etc., but fasten the eye to the beeswax by the aid of pins so that the cornea faces directly upwards and projects somewhat above the level of the water in the pan.

15. The Aqueous Humor and Anterior Chamber. Cut through the cornea at its junction with the sclerotic, and dissect it off completely. The liquid that escapes is the aqueous humor. It fills up the space between the cornea and the iris known as the anterior chamber of the eye.

16. Iris and Pupil. The iris is now completely exposed, and through its opening, the pupil, the anterior surface of the lens projects somewhat. Lift up the edge of the iris and notice its darkly pigmented posterior surface. This layer of pigment on the back of the iris is known as the *uvea*. It is continuous with the pigmented epithelium of the retina which is prolonged over the ciliary processes to the iris in the " pars ciliaris retinæ."

Lift up the iris with forceps, and cut it away at its junction with the choroid round its whole circumference.

17. The Ciliary Processes and the Suspensory Ligament. The anterior surface of the lens is now fully exposed, and the free edges of the ciliary processes lying on it. With the point of a seeker turn back the ciliary processes, and the suspensory ligament passing from the lens to the processes will be exposed. The ligament is too delicate to be seen easily, but if the lens is pushed somewhat outward it will be revealed.

18. The Capsule of the Lens. The suspensory ligament is attached directly to the capsule of the lens, which is a rather tough though transparent membrane enveloping the lens. If a bit of the anterior surface of the lens is pinched up with the forceps the capsule can be cut or broken through, and will peel off easily so that the lens can be slipped out. The capsule stays behind still attached to the ciliary processes by the suspensory ligament, and if the operation has been successfully performed a better view of the suspensory ligament will be obtained.

INDEX.

www.ingramcontent.com/pod-product-compliance
Lightning Source LLC
Chambersburg PA
CBHW030548270326
41927CB00008B/1560